I know Benny Proffitt. He would love to [...] who is rearing teenagers. He would love to coach and encourage those parents in the most demanding role they have this side of glory. Of course, there isn't time. So Benny has done the next best thing—he has shared his insights and encouragement in a book. Every parent will be blessed, especially as Benny details the seven powerful ways his own parents discipled and impacted his life for Christ. This is reading I easily recommend.

RICHARD ROSS, PH.D.
PROFESSOR OF STUDENT MINISTRY, SOUTHWESTERN SEMINARY;
AND SPOKESPERSON FOR THE INTERNATIONAL TRUE LOVE WAITS MOVEMENT

God has blessed Benny Proffitt with an abundance of wisdom, especially when it comes to the subject of parenting. This is one book that all parents should read before their child becomes a teenager. Youth pastors need, now more than ever, tools to help parents with their students. I am extremely proud that Benny slowed down enough to share his wisdom with us! His book is not a "how to" book but the reader can easily apply the seven basic principles outlined by Benny to their situation. I not only endorse Benny's new book, but I believe every youth pastor in America should be mandated to read and incorporate Benny's principles in their personal life as well as their ministry! Thank you, Benny, for hearing God's call on your life and for sharing your life with all of us.

DR. J. D. SIMPSON, JR.
AREA DIRECTOR OF FIRST PRIORITY OF SOUTH MISSISSIPPI

Benny Proffitt knows kids and he knows parents. After nearly four decades of supporting families as an educator, coach, minister, and most importantly a husband and dad, he has earned the right to speak to us as parents. My wife, Sandi, and I have allowed Benny and his wife, Marilou, to encourage, teach, and challenge us with their biblical example of parenting. I hope you will do the same in your quest to "chart the course" for you and your family.

GREG DAVIS
EXECUTIVE DIRECTOR OF FIRST PRIORITY OF ALABAMA

It has been a privilege to call Benny Proffitt my friend, but even more than that, he has been an example to me of a life sold out to the glory of God. His book is nothing more than a reflection of his life aim in calling students, adults, and families to be Christ followers. Whether you've been married for three years or fifty years; whether you are a single parent or in a blended family; this book will challenge you to 'praise Him to the next generation.' Through Scripture and practical wisdom Benny has gained during his lifetime, this book will call you to nothing more than what God desires from each of us—to be, look, and love like Jesus.

JASON GARRIS
MINISTER OF STUDENTS AT HERMITAGE HILLS BAPTIST CHURCH, HERMITAGE, TN

Charting the Course *is very unique among parenting materials. It profiles the value of a Christian heritage, defines the cultural crises we are facing, and presents a strategic plan for charting the course of parenting. The chapter layout is very readable and teachable. It's filled with the reality of the world we are facing, and the hope there is in Christ. God begins with us where we begin with Him.* Charting the Course *is a clear guide.*

DORIS HOWARD
FAMILY LIFE DIRECTOR, CENTRAL CHRISTIAN CHURCH, WICHITA, KS

In Charting the Course, *Benny Proffitt speaks from experience, credibility, and authenticity, reminding all parents what our first priorities need to be and how to stay the course God has called us to with those we love the most. As a parent, I'm always thankful for good training that helps me stay the course. Benny Proffitt's* Charting the Course *is a great resource for all moms and dads.*

BO BOSHERS
EXECUTIVE DIRECTOR OF STUDENT MINISTRY, WILLOW CREEK ASSOCIATION,
BARRINGTON, IL

charting
the course

the first priority of parenting

Benny Proffitt

Cover Design: Karen Phillips, Nashville, Tennessee

Interior Design: Sharon Collins of Artichoke Design, Nashville, Tennessee

Production Manager: Jacque Carrigan, Nashville, Tennessee

ISBN 978-9-76006-634-1 (trade paper)

Printed in the United States of America

05 06 07 08 Victor 9 8 7 6 5 4 3 2 1

table of contents

a note from the author

I feel blessed to be able to write this book for you. For the last thirty-seven years, I've been involved in full-time youth ministry, the first twenty-seven of which I was a youth pastor. The last ten years have been devoted to a national youth ministry I founded called First Priority of America. I've also been a high school teacher, and during my first eight years as a bivocational youth pastor, I coached high school basketball.

My experience in ministry and teaching exposed me to just about every good and bad thing parents could possibly do. I told them I would not try to tell them how to raise their children. But watching them surely taught me how to raise mine.

I can also speak to you from my own experience as the fortunate son of wonderful parents. At this writing, my mother is in her eighties and she still faithfully serves her church and her family. She is a living example of Christ every day and, in my opinion, will definitely have a front-row seat in heaven. My dad, who has gone to be with the Lord, was a devoted father who was the kind of dad every child should have. My fairly ideal world as a child doesn't prohibit me, though, from understanding what most parents are struggling with today, as I've been up close and personal with the struggles and pain within families for a long time.

Marilou is my beautiful wife of thirty-two years, and we have three amazing children. Two of my kids, Shawndee and BJ, are married, so I'm also blessed with a wonderful son-in-law, Jason, and daughter-in-law, Melissa. As the parents of our grandchildren, they are answers to our prayers. Joey is my college senior.

I leave the most fun for last—my grandson, Isaac, and granddaughter, Juliette. With more grandchildren on the way and many more promised, I am truly a blessed man.

As a dad, a husband, a teacher, and a minister, I want to share some of the lessons I've learned from my own successes and failures and from those of others.

The great truths I've received from these life experiences compel me to commit my life to becoming like Christ. I am compelled by my love for Him and my family to submit and commit to God's plan for my family and to partner with Him in raising my children. I know, in reality, they are His children.

Benny Proffitt

foreword
the Proffitt family speaks

So much of what is best in us is bound up in our love of family that it remains the measure of our stability because it measures our sense of loyalty. All other pacts of love or fear derive from it and are modeled upon it.
—HANIEL LONG, AMERICAN POET

Wilma Proffitt

Benny's mother, Wilma, is eighty-three, and has four children, ten grandchildren, and twelve great-grandchildren. After fifty years, she is still teaching Sunday school.

My husband and I were both born in a remote area of the Great Smoky Mountains in East Tennessee in the early 1920s. We were both blessed to have parents who were devoted to God, to each other, and to their children. Our parents worked hard to make sure we were provided for during the difficult years of the Great Depression in the 1930s. Even in the midst of tough times, we had a deep inner security of being loved.

Our parents nurtured the spiritual growth of their children. They instilled in us the importance of knowing about God and His Son Jesus, and the importance of putting our faith and trust into His care. From our parents, we learned the value of practicing tolerance and not being prejudiced or judgmental of others. My mother never talked disparagingly of anyone, and she expected the same from us.

When I wasn't at school, I worked alongside my mother every day and benefited from her wisdom and example. It wasn't until I had my own children that I realized how powerful and instructive that experience was for my parenting role.

When Joe and I were married on May 6, 1944, our goal was to establish a Christian home. For us, this meant daily study of God's Word and prayer time. In six years, we had four children. Joe and I dedicated our children to the Lord before they were born. Our utmost desire was to protect them from harm and to lead them in the ways of the Lord by truth and example. We prayed that they would grow up to love and serve the Lord.

As young parents, we knew that we could not rely on our own strength and good intentions. We prayed, listened to the Lord, and stayed in the Scripture. We found ourselves reading Psalms and Proverbs more often, and they became our guide for raising our children. Sunday school and church attendance were of utmost importance. Most of all, our children knew that Joe and I worked together and had the same goals.

We wanted our children to grow up with a sense of worth. We tried to help them develop self-esteem by encouraging their natural talents and special qualities and to help them understand other cultures and peoples. We endeavored to talk to them of many things—not talk at them. We loved reading to them daily, and we sang to them many old songs as well as new ones, instilling in them the love of music.

We welcomed and listened to their unique and varied ideas. Letting them experience the wide variety of their surroundings fed their natural curiosities and helped them develop an awareness of all life around them. We tried to kindle their imaginations, teach them to accept new ideas, and allow them time to dream.

Our aim was to be worthy examples for our children to follow, motivating them to achieve honest goals. We laughed with them and enjoyed our children, but we also prayed with them and offered unconditional love when life tested them. We did our best to be there for them—to celebrate their successes, understand their tears, soothe their disappointments, and calm their fears. We worked to share joys, inspire confidence, and help our children to accept defeat when it came, while keeping their eyes on their goals.

As their parents, we felt a God-given responsibility to be reverent and to hold certain values as sacred. We wanted them to be strong and secure in their faith and to ignore the doubters who could discourage them or lead them astray. We believed the biblical truth that if you teach your children how they should live, they will remember it all of their lives.

More than anything, we wanted our children to believe in themselves, to make right decisions, to take on the challenges of life, and to seek God's will. George W. Truett once said, "To know the will of God is the greatest knowledge; to do the will of God is the greatest achievement." We prayed that our children would be great achievers.

Our four children are treasures to us. Joe and I will be forever grateful to our heavenly Father for choosing us as their parents. Our prayer is that God will bless our family and that the Christian teachings Joe and I learned from our parents will be passed on for many generations. We have no fear for the future of our children, because early on we placed them into the care of our heavenly Father. God already has blessed us with ten grandchildren, ten great-grandchildren, and there are two more on the way.

When the world makes parents feel unworthy, we must remember that a hundred years from now it will not matter what was in our bank account, what sort of house we lived in, or the kind of car we drove. What will matter is that the world will be different because we were important in the lives of our children.

Marilou Proffitt

Marilou and Benny have been married for thirty-two years. Marilou teaches fourth grade in public school.

As a young girl growing up in a Christian home, I committed my life to serving Christ. I prayed for God to give me a Christian husband

and dreamed about having a Christian home to raise children of my own who would also love and want to serve God. I didn't know then just how much God was listening and how well He would answer my prayer.

One of my first conversations with Benny, after we met in college, was about our shared desire to serve the Lord and have a Christian family of our own someday. As we dated, we talked about many things—we wondered if we would get married, and we had fun dreaming about what our children might be like. We liked to kiss too! We talked a lot about marriage being not just between two people but the coming together of two worlds. We discussed how the influence of our parents and our past family experiences would affect our decisions and the way we would raise our children. We were fortunate to have parents who loved and cared for us, but since there are no perfect families, we wanted to repeat only the good things and eliminate the not-so-good things.

When we married and began our journey together, our dependence on God became more important than ever. Suddenly, we were dealing with the pressures of married life, trying to reach young people for Christ, and beginning a family of our own. We discussed our fears of bringing children into this rapidly changing and seemingly degenerating society, but I decided that if God could guide me through the turbulent years of the '60s and '70s, He would be there for my children no matter what their future challenges would be. We believed Jesus was the answer, and we trusted Him to be the answer for our children.

One thing we have rediscovered over and over is that God is faithful. We tried to do our part to point our children to Jesus, and Jesus has definitely done His part to draw our children to Himself, His salvation, and His ways.

We worked very hard to bring the best of our two worlds together into one marriage, with Christ being in the center. We are grateful to our parents, who stayed true to their wedding vows, 'til death parted them. My parents were married for sixty-eight years, and Benny's parents were married for fifty-nine years, before both our fathers died about three years ago. We are committed to leaving our children the same legacy of faithfulness to each other and redeeming faith in our Lord that was passed on to us by our parents.

Let me challenge and encourage you to leave your children a legacy of faithfulness and the promise of hope that can only be found in Jesus Christ.

Shawndee Proffitt LoVoy

Benny and Marilou's daughter, Shawndee, is twenty-eight and lives with her husband, Jason. They have two children, Isaac and Juliette, and are expecting their third child. Shawndee was a fourth-grade teacher prior to becoming a full-time mom.

As I reflect on the impact my parents' walk with the Lord has had on my life, the prevailing thought that comes to mind is the feeling of unconditional love and acceptance that is with me every day. Knowing that I always had a place to go where I was fully accepted made it easy for me to understand God's love and acceptance. As I grow older and develop deeper relationships with others, I realize that not everyone lives their daily life feeling they are worthy of love. This affects their relationship with the Lord, with others, and with their own children.

I see how my experience of unconditional love positively affects my husband and my children, and I realize the importance of what my parents gave me. Through this love, I have freedom—freedom to fail, freedom to be vulnerable, and freedom to offer this kind of love to my own family. I now understand that Jesus Christ loves me freely, and it's not dependent on how good or worthy I am of His love. This knowledge has changed my heart and allowed me to desire Him and the life He desires me to live.

I'm not saying my parents were perfect or that I haven't had struggles. We all learned and grew together. But love was never in question.

I could name many practical ways my parents discipled me, but they all fall under the umbrella of unconditional love and acceptance that ultimately pointed me to a Savior who loves and accepts me eternally.

BJ Proffitt

Benny and Marilou's son BJ is twenty-six and lives with his wife, Melissa. He is a medical physicist at Vanderbilt University Medical Center. They are expecting their first child.

When I think about my childhood, I don't remember anything especially negative. I have so many friends who look back and wince, but I had no traumatic experiences or major wounds. Growing up was pretty easy for me.

I do, however, remember many positive things. Dad was not only my father but also my youth minister and sports coach. I remember summer youth camps, weekend retreats, and hours in the gym shooting baskets and perfecting ball-handling drills. I grew up watching Dad's competitiveness in sports, his guitar skills, and his desire to accomplish goals at work. These are the things that have motivated my own achievements. My father and I now share in each other's successes.

Mom was not only my mother but also my teacher. Her classroom was always right down the hall in school. It was the place where I learned to value her teaching. My mother and I share a perfectionist nature.

As with most children, my perception of God was formed by my parents—most significantly by my father. As I grew and learned more, I had no problem believing in God and trusting Him. I think the main reason was that for my parents, God was real—not just at church or in front of the crowd but also at home. A day didn't go by without Dad pointing to God's presence in our home.

I'm not saying everything was picture-perfect. My parents made mistakes and so did I. Dad could get angry when my brother, sister, or I was disobedient. I gained a lot of secondhand experience from the discipline of my siblings. My ears were always open to what was being said in the next room. I often felt our parents were being unfair, but as we aged, their rules from our childhood transitioned more into guidelines. We had the freedom to make our own choices, having been taught that life always has consequences.

It really hits me now that, in all the years at home, church, or anywhere in public, I can't remember one time when my parents were fake or they put on a show. It's because of that honesty and integrity I have developed so much respect for them. As an adult, my relationship with them has become one of friendship.

The greatest gift my parents gave me, besides their faith in Christ, was the ability to move out into the world with confidence. I knew when I left home I was ready for independence, for marriage, and for being a parent one day.

Joey Proffitt

Benny and Marilou's son Joey is twenty-two and a senior at Samford University.

There are so many things about my parents that make them different. It's not the things they do that make them different, it's who they are. I recognize that most when I see other parents.

I've noticed three different types of relationships my friends have with their parents that just don't work. First, I have friends whose parents are overly strict. You would think these kids would be the most obedient, but they are, in fact, the ones who live secret lives, trying not to get caught. They have broken relationships with their parents and avoid them whenever possible. It's not that I didn't fear my parents or their punishment of me; I respected them because I knew their character, even behind closed doors, and the example they were setting for me. I wanted to live up to their example.

Second, I have friends whose parents are more concerned about being buddies than parents. These parents let my friends get away with anything, in essence saying, "Kids will be kids." The problem occurs when they do have to be parents, and their kids don't respect them. It's different with my parents—because of who they are, I want to be their friend, and they didn't have to sacrifice their role as my parent. My parents are fun to be around for the most part. But now that I'm not under their roof, I realize I didn't need more buddies—I had plenty of those—I needed parents. They don't seem like my bosses; they're my mentors.

Finally, I have friends who have Christian parents who go to church and help others, just like mine. These friends live in loving homes and, for the most part, are good kids. They never got involved in sex or drugs, and their parents made sure they were in church and that they were obedient. But they don't desire a relationship with Jesus. The older they are and the more freedom they get, the more they fall away. They know what they're supposed to do, but they continually ask why.

The reason that I respect my parents and why we are friends is because I know why they are the way they are. They are sinners saved by grace and live lives seeking a relationship with Christ. It wasn't that we prayed before every meal and at every bedtime—we didn't. It wasn't because we had a time set apart every day for family Bible study—we didn't. It wasn't because we didn't have arguments—we did and I still think I was right on every one. I grew up seeing my parents seek the Lord in Bible study, in prayer, and in serving others. I saw how they loved each other, their own parents, and all other people. Their love showed me how my sister, brother, and I were more important than any worldly thing. They were understanding, yet honest; forgiving, yet tough. They were real! And most importantly, they told me and showed why they are the way they are. They lived the truth they tried to teach me.

introduction

During my life's work, I've rallied closely with divorced parents, drug-addicted parents, and parents who have abused and even abandoned their children. I've worked with parents who have committed adultery and who have been in prison for murder. But in all my years of ministry, I have never met a person who wanted to fail as a parent. Of course, we all fail to some degree—some of us fail miserably—but I've never met a parent who wanted to see their children fail in life, even if they provided little or no potential for their children to succeed.

I believe the primary role of a parent is to develop their children into disciples—people devoted to becoming like Jesus Christ. We must lead our children to become God's children, to take on the very nature of their heavenly Father the way Jesus did. We are preparing them to serve God in this world. But more importantly, we are preparing them to serve God in His heavenly kingdom.

We must teach our children what is true and right, and we will be held accountable to God for how faithful we are in our responsibility to deliver His message. The Scripture proclaims that anyone who leads even one of the little ones (our children) astray will be held to a greater judgment (Matthew 18:5–6). Misusing this critical role of teaching children greatly displeases God. For this reason, it is a sobering responsibility to be a parent.

My friend Mike Roberts once told me, "I believe parenting is the most important job we'll ever have and the one we are least prepared to do." So I wrote this book to help prepare you for your role and responsibilities as a parent and the great opportunity you have in impacting the world through your children. If you take what you learn here and put it into action, your children will have the correct model to follow, and they will develop the confidence to follow you as you follow Christ.

Before We Get Started

I want to address the different types of parents who will be reading this book, as no one is excluded from these lessons on the basis of marital or family status. Because we live in a vastly shifting culture, there are four types of parents today:

1. Married parents who jointly share in the raising of their children (traditional parents)
2. Divorced parents who jointly share in the raising of their children (co-parents)
3. Parents who raise their children alone (single parents)
4. Married parents who, for a variety of reasons, must raise their children alone (solo parents)

Please know that whatever your situation might be, your parenting abilities are no less effective because of your situation. Although there are many fine examples of married couples who successfully raise their children, some single, solo, and co-parents do a much better job at parenting than a lot of married couples who attempt to do it together. It's not God's intention that you should parent alone, but He certainly doesn't abandon anyone who puts their faith in Him. In fact, quite the opposite is true—God says He will become the Father to the fatherless. He will personally stand in the gap of any shortfall. Your prayer and mine for your children is that through your influence and leadership, these lessons will help them become wonderful, Godlike parents. I pray with you that they will find a lifelong God-centered mate and not have to go through the difficulties you have faced as single and solo parents.

About the Book

Charting the Course isn't an especially large book, but we'll cover a lot of ground.

Part One is called THE VISION, and it has four chapters:

1. A VIEW OF THE ROAD AHEAD – This is a very basic overview of what to expect while you read this book.
2. NATURAL VS. SUPERNATURAL PARENTING – It's tempting to look inside yourself for answers and make decisions based on your own strength. This chapter will help you identify ways to stop relying on yourself for answers and start depending on God as the Lord of your family and your life.
3. FOLLOWING A WELL-TRAVELED ROAD – I owe much to my parents for their Godlike leadership; this chapter will help you understand why it's so important to have mentors and quality leadership examples to follow while raising your kids.
4. THE BATTLE PLAN – This chapter contains everything you'll need to go into battle and win the souls of your children.

Part Two is called THE EXPEDITION, and it's the instructional part of this book that teaches you how to become God-centered parents to your children. Each chapter in this section covers the seven pursuits of godly parents. The final chapter will help you take an inventory of what you've learned and offer support to you as you continue the exciting expedition ahead of you.

There's also much more in general to this book:

- First and foremost, each chapter will show us what the Bible says about preparing our children to serve God.
- We'll discover the way discipleship works between parents and their children.
- We'll discuss why parents feel inadequate to disciple their children.
- We'll find out why taking your children to church isn't enough.

- In many of the chapters, you'll interact with this book through exercises called "Check Points" that are placed throughout the text for you to stop and answer questions, fill in the blanks, and journal your thoughts. Think of these Check Points as rest stops along the journey, where you can take a break, reflect on the path behind and before you, and take an inventory of your supplies.

> *Churches should empower families, not replace them.*

- You'll also find many "Notes from Benny's Journal." These highlight some of my personal experiences and observations I've gathered over the years. They'll offer valuable insight into many aspects of parenting and discipleship.
- Even though we'll talk about what to do in our spiritual journey and how to do it, we'll focus on understanding and staying focused on the why. (If we don't remind ourselves why we are spending the time and energy it takes to nurture our spiritual life, what to do and how to do it will be meaningless, routine activities.)
- Lastly, you'll find review, teaching, and discussion questions at the end of some chapters. These are powerful tools for individual review or for group participation.

The bottom line is that you have the responsibility of discipling your children, but at the same time you must faithfully allow yourself to be discipled. The two go hand in hand.

Read this book and share its lessons with your children, family, and friends. Use it as a resource for your Bible study, cell group, or Sunday school class. Let's pursue God on this journey through life, in order to find real and eternal life in Jesus Christ.

Let's partner with God to inspire and guide our children so they'll join us as we chart the course of this adventurous journey toward home.

part one
the vision

"LET'S THINK OF OUR JOURNEY TOWARD
CHRISTLIKENESS AS A CONTINUOUSLY
MOVING TRAIN, HEADING FOR A GREAT
CITY WHERE THE TRACK WILL END."

a view of the road ahead

what does good parenting look like?

The answer to this question is a journey that must begin with an understanding of the ultimate purpose for which God originally made human beings. He reveals the answer in Genesis 1:26–27:

> *Then God said, "Let Us make man in Our image, according to Our likeness; let them have dominion over the fish of the sea, over the birds of the air, and over the cattle, over all the earth and over every creeping thing that creeps on the earth." So God created man* in His own image; *in the image of God He created him; male and female He created them.* (NKJV; emphasis added)

We know that all of creation was made to show God's greatness—His glory. But in Genesis 1:26–27, we see He made us for a special purpose—to be *like* Him and to *reflect* His image.

Because of their sin, Adam and Eve lost the reflection of God's image, which, of course, affected us too. Adam and Eve introduced sin into the world and, according to Romans 3:23, we have all sinned and fallen short of the glory or image of God. But God's purpose for us was not lost!

His end goal is still for us to be like Him, and He desires that we grow in our understanding of our salvation and all that it means to be saved. But salvation is so much more than going to heaven when we die. It is restoration of what was lost. The Book of Romans says it is His glory, or likeness, that we lose when we sin, but His glory is restored in salvation, where God not only offers us forgiveness and the promise of heaven, but also everything we need to be restored to His image—to become like Him.

Made to Reflect the Visible Image of the Invisible God

One of the best ways to inspire hunger for progress toward any goal is to provide a clear picture of the goal. Since God wants us to have His nature, one of the best things He can do for us is to give us a picture of who He is. But what would a picture of the invisible God of creation look like? The perfect image of God is found in Jesus Christ, who was, as Colossians 1:15 says, the visible image of the invisible God. And Hebrews 1:3 tells us that Christ was the exact representation of God's nature.

So God's plan is for us to reflect His image and character, and His plan from the beginning was to make that happen through Jesus Christ. Throughout the Bible, God repeats His promise to fulfill this goal. Romans 8:28–29 was revealed to the apostle Paul on his journey toward Christlikeness:

And we know that all things work together for good to those who love God, to those who are the called according to His purpose. For whom He foreknew, He also predestined to be conformed to the image of His Son, that He might be the firstborn among many brethren. (NKJV)

Notes from Benny's Journal
"A ROMANS EPIPHANY"

Early in my ministry, when the truth of Romans 8 became personal to me, it changed my life. I realized that God's purpose and destiny for me was much more than going to heaven when I die. I have seen so many Christians who live meaningless lives— simply trying to survive, going through the motions of Christian living, and just waiting around until they go to heaven.

Life, for me, became a meaningful, exciting adventure when I began to understand that God wanted to use everything I experienced, day by day, to make me more like Him. It was then that my attitude about everyday earthly life changed. I realized that every encounter and experience of my life was an opportunity for me to become more like Christ. No matter if it was good or bad, God wanted to work through that situation to build His character in me and to accomplish His purposes through me.

How I responded to every valley and every victory would either reflect Christ in me or it would reveal my self-centered, stubborn, foolish pride. Learning to listen to the Holy Spirit, as He convinced me of right and convicted me of wrong, became a crucial part of my transforming journey with Jesus.

The most important thing parents must do before they can expect to nurture Christlikeness in their children is to become God-centered by their daily example of humble submission to God's authority and their complete trust in His love.

You see, Jesus didn't die merely for our admission to glory, however wonderful that is. He lived and died for us so we could reflect the likeness of God the way He did (see John 17:22–26). Remember when Philip asked Jesus to show him and the other disciples the Father? Jesus replied that everyone who has seen Him has seen the Father (John 14:9). Jesus was the visible image of the invisible God (Colossians 1:15). Jesus was the personification of God's nature (Colossians 1:19). Everything Jesus did, every word He spoke, His every thought was an outgrowth of God the Father *in* Him.

> *The real destination of our lives isn't just a place; it's a person—Jesus.*

Ultimately, heaven is going to be heavenly because we'll be with Jesus. But it will also be heavenly because we'll be with countless other people who are *like* Jesus. So the real destination of our lives isn't just a *place*; it's a *person*—Jesus Himself, who has an eternal purpose for us long before we see Him face-to-face and even before we see heaven as it fully is (1 Corinthians 2:9).

Discipleship Is a Journey with Jesus

Let's think of our journey toward Christlikeness as a continuously moving train, heading for a great city where the track will end:

The city is heaven—the fulfillment of God's promise that we will be with Him forever and be conformed into the likeness of Jesus.

The train is our life in Christ.

The track is God's plan, which He lays out for us to travel in trusting obedience to Him.

The conductor of the train is Jesus; we have to trust Him because we can't see the track all the time and that makes us feel lost.

The engine of this train is the Holy Spirit, who gives us the power to put our faith and trust in the One who is calling us to keep moving down the track.

A strong faith allows us to rest in God's assurance that He is on the journey with us and we will arrive at the promised destination.

Sometimes we're on board this journey as passengers; other times, we're the crew. And then there are times when we *think* we're the conductor, but, again, our faith in what Jesus has already done and promises to do in us is the true power behind the journey. When we take control—with our self-assurance, independent ambition, or anything else that weakens our submission to Jesus—we put the train in danger of jumping the track.

Solomon tells us that some people even cut their journey short by their persistent foolishness, insisting on driving their own lives

(Ecclesiastes 7:17). But usually a derailed Christian life just means a lesson learned, even if it's a hard lesson.

If you are anything in this analogy about the train, you are *sometimes* the leader of the crew that gives direction and encouragement to your children. In addition, you are always a fellow passenger on the train as you continue to trust the conductor, Jesus Christ. You are to cooperate with God in building your children's faith in Him. You don't own the train, God does. You didn't provide the engine; God did. But He has given you His Word—a set of instructions to follow for your part in training the crew and fellow passengers. You must depend on God's plans to bring your children's faith to life and set them on their journey. Believe it or not, He wants that even more than you do.

The Family's Role in God's Plan

In this life, God calls us to accomplish many things in His name. But God's first priority is for us to become like Jesus. How that happens involves a lot of things and a lot of people, the most influential of whom are parents, and the most influential place is the family.

Pursuing God above all else is a daily part of our journey. How do we confidently meet the challenge to impact our children without living in bondage to our inevitable mistakes? This question makes praying over our children, studying His Word, and depending on God all the more important. We need God's grace to cover our children and protect their hearts from permanently reflecting all the broken things they will inevitably see in us.

This fundamental aspect of parenting should give you the correct impression that discipling your children has more to do with being discipled yourself than personally bringing about change in your children. An unaccountable life is not worth living. We need to learn to see ourselves as God sees us in order to be better disciplers of our children.

More than once, Jesus explained to His disciples that everything He did was

An unaccountable life is not worth living.

in obedience to the Father and not the works of His own power and authority (John 5:19). Earlier God spoke through the Old Testament prophet Zechariah, saying that what He wanted to accomplish would be accomplished and that it would be done: *"'Not by might nor by power, but by My Spirit,' Says the* LORD *of hosts"* (Zechariah 4:6 NKJV).

Jesus showed us what dependence on the Father is and how it is lived out: by faith. As faithful parents and stewards of children who belong to God, let's diligently offer ourselves to be used for God's purposes each day, just like Jesus did. Let's pray that we won't become weary in well-doing, and that we'll entrust the future to God. If we do these things, our children will more likely do the same.

> *Discipleship is not a meeting with a manual. Discipleship is a journey with Jesus.*

Jesus said, "Follow me!" A disciple is not just a person who knows Jesus, but a person who desires to become *like* Jesus and then pursues Him as the most important thing in his or her life. It's God's plan that parents be the main source that inspires children to live as disciples of Christ.

So many parents take their kids to church, sign them up for classes and programs, and think that will make their kids disciples of Christ. But discipleship is not just about attending meetings at church and completing workbooks. I like to tell people, "Discipleship is not a meeting with a manual. Discipleship is a journey with Jesus." It's an everyday adventure for those who've chosen Christ as their Savior and Lord.

Notes from Benny's Journal
"WHO'S IN CHARGE?"

When I became a dad, I had been involved in ministry long enough to know I couldn't depend on church programs, a special book, or other people to disciple my children. I haven't been a perfect parent, but over the years I learned a lot about how to disciple my own children by observing other parents. There were many great parents who served as my role models. I also saw parents who had worldly priorities, which resulted in great struggles and heartache with their children.

*As a youth pastor in a church with more than a thousand teenagers, I told parents I wasn't there to disciple their kids. Instead, I told them **they** were given the authority and responsibility by God to disciple them. My purpose was to be there to encourage, equip, and support them with tools in the form of teaching, guidance, and programs for their kids. They had the God-given privilege and responsibility of being the hands-on, day-to-day disciplers. Since God's first priority is for us to become like Jesus, then a parent's first priority is to lead his or her children to Christ and get them on the path that leads them to Christlikeness.*

A lot of parents don't understand that they are *partners* with God; He has given them the keys to the kingdom. Parents get to decide what is beneficial to faith building in their children's lives. The enemies of the gospel certainly know this, which is why the family, in general, and parental authority, in particular, are under attack in our society.

This brings us to the next thing parents must do—recognize that we are in a battle for the hearts, minds, and future of our kids.

Many of my baby boom generation are deceived and live in fear because of negative experiences as children in our families and churches. To a large extent, religion was either forced down our throats or it played no significant role in our development. Compared to previous generations, baby boomers were more influenced by cultural values than we were by our parents' values. As a result, many of our own children have built their lives on the lies of this world, instead of the truth of God's Word.

Those of us who fear making mistakes as parents must overcome that fear with faith in God. He is in control, and He has promised to be our helper as we disciple our children with His wisdom and faithfulness.

God also desires that we, as His personal possessions, prosper in all we do and live lives of fulfillment. But God doesn't even let His own desire for those things get in the way of fulfilling His *first* priority, which

> *Commit your way to the LORD, Trust also in Him, And He shall bring it to pass. He shall bring forth your righteousness as the light, And your justice as the noonday (Psalm 37:5–6 NKJV).*

is to conform us to the image of His Son, Jesus Christ (Romans 8:29).

Here is another reason why this is so important to God: children in a family are supposed to be like their father (Ephesians 5:1–2). Just as Jesus wants to bring glory to His Father, God wants to bring glory to His Son and present to Him a perfect family, a glorious bride. The Church of Jesus Christ is called "the Bride of Christ" and the family of God. We help prepare each of our children to be a part of God's holy, heavenly family. Could there be any greater calling or purpose in parenting?

Wisdom for the Journey

We've established three things on our vision quest thus far:

1. God made us for a very specific purpose.
2. We must accept responsibility for discipling our children.
3. There are obstacles we will inevitably face and overcome.

But how do we do it?

We need broadly applied wisdom from God to disciple our children well. James tells us that God is faithful to give wisdom to anyone who asks (James 1:5). God provides that wisdom in a variety of ways, but He is always the source of *true* wisdom. We'll find it in His Word, in His presence as He answers prayer, and in the counsel of Christ-centered people He puts in our paths.

Set aside prayerful time alone with God and His Word every day. The amount of time isn't as important as simply making it a habit. Your hunger for God's presence and His Word will grow as you nurture the habit of meeting with Him.

Pray for and seek out God-centered mentors who can speak to the challenges you face. God is ready to give you wisdom, but He wants you to ask Him for it and then look for it! The Spirit is the doorway to wisdom, and the key that unlocks that door is a humble, submissive heart that worships God as Father and King.

You're reading this book for a reason: you're looking for answers, hope, and fellowship with God. I pray that what you discover in the following chapters will breathe new life into your journey as a disciple and a discipler.

check point

The goal of this book is to help you see what it means to be like God, and to increase your hunger to reflect His image and His character.

Forget how much like God you *hope* you are right now. Imagine that Jesus suddenly appears physically to you, and He tells you that He wants to personally disciple you. He says He will come to you often throughout each day, plus whenever you call on Him. He will teach you, encourage you, inspire you, and, yes, even rebuke you when necessary. He promises to do this for as many years as it takes for others to see Him when they look at you. But you must never claim that you are special just because He is doing this for you. He is already doing the same thing for all other believers, but without appearing to them physically.

Think about what this experience would be like if it started today, and then imagine what other people will see in you ten years from now. What will they see, for instance, when they look at how you love; how you relate to people you like; how you relate to people you don't like; how you deal with conflict and pain; how you evaluate opportunities; and what you do with success and failure?

As you imagine what you will be like, don't filter out your own personality as though you don't exist. Remember, it is *you* who are reflecting God's image, not some washed-out, hyper-religious version of you. Also, don't imagine you have achieved perfect Christlikeness either. Instead, imagine how Jesus has helped you to deal with your dusty places that will probably always be part of you. Look at yourself after ten years of unbroken intimacy with Jesus, and in the space below, write what you see. Be as specific and honest as you can.

For Review, Teaching, or Discussion

Think for a moment about what you've read in this first chapter. Take a few minutes to write down a few words in the space below that summarize this chapter and the most important message you derived from it.

How does God feel about our children?

1. God wants our children to be like _____.
2. Discipling children is a parent's _____ priority.

3. Discipleship is our journey with_____.

4. Parents are partners with _____.

5. God will give us _____to parent our children.

6. Parenting is a _____.

7. God will be your perfect example as a _____.

natural vs. supernatural parenting

how can I find real power to lead my children to successful lives?

A VIEW OF THE ROAD AHEAD:

- *Understanding the difference between natural and supernatural parenting*
- *Turning away from natural parenting*
- *Identifying true spiritual maturity*
- *Learning to let God lead in Spirit and wisdom*

Even though we know where our true home lies, our lives in this world aren't *just* about preparing for heaven. There are things God has for us to do in this world as well.

God's Word gives us a command to share His message with all men, and the message is that God loves them and desires for them to be made complete. Jesus prayed, *"Thy kingdom come. Thy will be done in earth, as it is in heaven"* (Matthew 6:10 KJV). And, as we know, God's kingdom is in the hearts and lives of His people.

Naturally, the fruit we desire most is that our children will live successful lives. We can call our own lives successful if we live in a way that inspires our children to live for God. But when we become parents, we soon learn—if we didn't know it before—that we don't have power over our children the way God does. We don't have enough strength and wisdom to ensure continual peace in our homes or perfect progress in our children's journeys toward Godlike adulthoods. Raising God-centered children in a fallen world that seems bent on corrupting them is impossible for us to manage on our own. In fact, in our natural state, *we* will be the main corrupting influence, no matter how much we love our children. We need supernatural strength and wisdom to truly please God as parents and to successfully raise children to become adults who love, forgive, serve, work, worship, and live like Christ.

God's goal through your leadership as parents is to transform your children's natural self-importance into God-fearing, Christ-centered, Holy Spirit-controlled maturity.

But despite what the Bible tells us about what God wants, there are many compassionate people around us who don't put their hope in God's earthly kingdom. They don't know God personally through Jesus, so they don't hope for anything better than life in this world. Some of these people spend their lives laboring to make the world more just and peaceful, because they have no other hope. Their consciousness about the need is good; they seem to know instinctively that we are stewards of creation and ministers of justice to one another, but they attempt to bring justice and peace to the world by their own strength, without acknowledging whose world this is.

Of all the things this life is supposed to teach us, chief among them is the fact that God is in charge—there is no one above Him, and He has no equals. All sin begins by saying, "I reject God's will and authority over me in favor of my own will." God's goal through your leadership as parents is to transform your children's natural self-importance into God-fearing, Christ-centered, Holy Spirit-controlled maturity.

For the rest of this chapter, let's look at three things:

1. The difference between natural versus supernatural parenting.
2. How we can be parents who are influenced less by our flesh and more by the Spirit of God.
3. How to understand and enter the battle within ourselves that we must face as Christian parents.

Natural Parenting: How We Lead Without Partnership with God

Throughout the Bible, we are told that in order to serve God we must deny ourselves, which means to put away our own agenda and trust the road God wants us to travel. But we live in a culture where everything is about self-improvement, self-reliance, rugged individualism, and fulfilling one's dreams. These aren't bad things in and of themselves until they become more about self-glorification than personal responsibility and living freely.

If you are going to be a greater influence on your children than the culture, your children need to learn to trust your leadership more than they trust the culture.

The unfortunate thing is that our children are, to a great extent, products of our culture. They learn to be self-centered by connecting with a culture of self-interest as their main influence. If you are going to be a greater influence on your children than the culture, your children need to learn to trust your leadership more than they trust the culture. And you will not be trustworthy until you deny your own agendas and self-interest and learn to trust the leading of God's Spirit.

We Lead Naturally by the Flesh

Most people suddenly begin learning a great deal about selfless love from the moment they hold their own child for the first time.

Everything suddenly revolves around the child and what the child wants and needs. But as a child grows, parents can become weary and begin to lose patience; and if the child doesn't perform as expected, parents may become dissatisfied with the rising discomfort in their lives that the child represents. Unconditional love becomes more difficult to extend. Without the spirit of gentleness and self-control, parents may respond in ways that bring condemnation on the child. Such responses to threats and offenses always come out of the flesh and not the Spirit.

We don't want to be Pharisees, but that is what we can become when we parent in the flesh. We can be very clear about enforcing rules for our children, but if that's all we do, we'll alienate our children. Rules without relationship produce rebellion.[1] At the same time, relationship without rules will also alienate children.

Without rules and parental supervision, children become insecure and feel undervalued. The damage this causes to their self-esteem can produce even worse rebellion. Teenagers will sometimes even break the law in order to get their parents to act on their behalf. They may not even know why they would do such things, but children often become lawless because they have a deep hunger to be shown who they are and that what they do matters to their parents. Both extremes of parenting in the flesh produce alienated children.

Rules without relationship produce rebellion; at the same time, relationship without rules will also alienate children.

The flesh only knows how to gather information. It then rules from knowledge and emotion and produces Pharisees who are judging and condemning. But the Holy Spirit speaks to our hearts and minds, producing a heart of love and a mind with the wisdom of God—the mind of Christ. The transforming power of God gives us a new heart and a new mind.

Parenting in the natural is usually about dos and don'ts. The flesh tends to demand perfection, because it fears what it can't control. Paul says that

[1] Josh McDowell and Bob Hostetler, *Beyond Belief to Conviction*, Tyndale House Publishers, 2002.

the demands of the law stir our sin nature to rebel (Romans 7:8). So natural parenting in the flesh will only produce rebellion in our children. Even if they don't act out or resist our demands, they can develop a rebellious heart of resentment that they might carry into adulthood.

Our natural rebellion isn't because we fear change; it's because we naturally fear and resent being controlled. Being controlled means we are giving up our own will, and we naturally want to make sure we get what we want. If children don't learn to trust the leadership of Spirit-led parents by the time they are young adults, they'll have a hard time yielding to the leading of the Holy Spirit as adults. Many years of disappointment with their own agenda will probably be necessary before they give up and let the Spirit of God lead them.

Now you know why Jesus came to give us His life and to save our souls. You can see what nonsense it is to have a reborn spirit that is alive in Christ but then continue to live life with a dying soul that isn't yielded to the source of life. This is the reason why many Christians are suffering and why there is so much personal and family dysfunction among Christians.

The Most Divisive Issue

There has always been a lot of controversy between churches and denominations about the role of the Holy Spirit in Christians' lives. But there is a much sadder reality in our churches than just our lack of unity about the work of the Holy Spirit. Our views of the Holy Spirit have become, for some, a measure of spiritual superiority. Many churches look upon other churches as unenlightened or spiritually immature because they don't practice their ideology of the Holy Spirit.

Notes from Benny's Journal
"NO ONE IS IMMUNE"

In the church where I grew up, we didn't talk much about the Holy Spirit. This may have been due to fear of being out of control or fear that comes from the lack of under-

standing about the work of the Holy Spirit. It's interesting that God sent His Spirit to unite us but this has been the most divisive issue in the body of Christ.

I've been in numerous discussions about this with groups of Christian leaders from different denominations and ministries, and I hear comments that sound so superior and judgmental. So I'll ask, "How many of you have had ministers in your denominations or organizations leave their churches because they were caught in some kind of immoral conduct?" They all admit that this tragedy has occurred in all their organizations.

The obvious next question is, "How many of you have seen families broken up in your churches through crisis and divorce?" I'll get the same answer.

Finally I'll ask, "How many of you have had kids brought up in your churches that end up lost, broken, and even abandoning the faith?" Everyone admits they have.

I then make my point, saying, "I think we can all agree that it is the work of the Holy Spirit that makes us like Christ. So if a church really practiced a theology of the Holy Spirit that is superior to all other churches, it wouldn't be having the same problems that all other churches have."

If one church's theology is superior, then that church and its members' lives should be superior, right? I've never known of a church where that was true.

Spiritual maturity does not bring spiritual superiority. Spiritual

> *Spiritual maturity does not bring spiritual superiority. Spiritual maturity produces humility.*

maturity produces humility. In other words, in Christ you work your way to the bottom, not the top. As you mature spiritually, you don't work your way to spiritual superiority so you can say, "I've got the truth and you don't." Maturity makes you a servant of all people. No one and no church has an entirely correct theology.

I am grateful that when God forgives all our sins in Christ, He forgives our theological errors as well. No Christian lives a perfectly pure life in the Spirit. We all stumble under the influence of our flesh—our fallen, self-centered nature. Part of what God is doing in our lives is training us to walk more and more in the power of His Spirit.

Answering the Question

Remember the question at the beginning of this chapter?

How can I find real power to lead my children to successful lives?

It doesn't take superior theology. What is necessary is a daily, moment-by-moment submission to the Holy Spirit that takes time to develop. It's a process. Like a tree, the more we are refreshed by the streams of God's living water, the richer and more abundant will be the fruit our children will see us bear in our lives.

My prayer is that our children's generation of Christians will become the church—God's people. I pray they will operate in the unity reflected in the Father, Son, and Holy Spirit that was prayed for by Christ Himself in John 17:20–23:

> *"I do not pray for these alone, but also for those who will believe in Me through their word; that they all may be one, as You, Father, are in Me, and I in You; that they also may be one in Us, that the world may believe that You sent Me. And the glory which You gave Me I have given them, that they may be one just as We are one: I in them, and You in Me; that they may be made perfect in one, and that the world may know that You have sent Me, and have loved them as You have loved Me"* (NKJV).

Supernatural Parenting:
How God Leads in Partnership with Us

There is only one perfect parent—God Himself. God revealed Himself as a Father and shows us a picture of His perfect love in the story of the prodigal son in chapter 15 of the Gospel of Luke. Everyone knows this story, but most people think the story is about the prodigal son. Jesus was actually teaching us about the nature and character of His heavenly Father.

The loving father of the prodigal son freely let his child go, knowing he might squander his inheritance. The father knew his son could possibly fall into evil hands, but hoped that he would one day return to his father's love. The father waited and watched for his son and was the first to see the prodigal stumbling home. He didn't even wait to hear his son's repentance but ran to him, celebrating the opportunity to love the son who had been "dead" but was alive again. What an accurate portrayal of our sinful nature and a beautiful picture of God's redeeming love for us!

The son came home because he remembered his father's loving and forgiving character. In his home, the son had always seen justice tempered with mercy. He remembered that his father showed the same charity to his servants that he did to his family. Likewise, our children know if we have a heart of encouragement or condemnation, and they know if we are consistent in our character and conduct. They know if we are the same people at church that we are at home; they probably know if we are the same people in our workplace as well.

God Leads Supernaturally by the Spirit

It's amazing how much can be overcome by approaching our parenting challenges with the Word of God and the voice of the Spirit. In Christ we are made alive by God's Spirit. It follows then that we should follow very closely the source of our life in everything we do (Galatians 5:25). We need to pray continually, "Lord, I need Your Spirit right now in this situation. Please guide me." We must take a stand that we will live and parent our children according to the Spirit of God and not according to our fleshly human nature.

The Bible says that when we commit our lives to Christ, He gives us a gift, and that gift is His Holy Spirit. The Spirit isn't just *with* us; He actually *lives in* us. The Spirit is what gives us life. Ephesians 1:13–14 says the Spirit is God's mark of ownership on us; it's His seal. If the Holy Spirit is not in you, you're not His. So if you are a believer, then you have received the Holy Spirit as a gift from God.

The Book of Acts records the beginnings of the church, but the story is really about the acts of the Holy Spirit. I'm not sure if Christians will ever agree on whether the Holy Spirit still works miracles like those recorded in Acts 2, 5, 19, and 28. But we must trust that God still reigns and rules in the church and in the world through the Holy Spirit.

The Holy Spirit was sent by Christ to live in His followers, as the Church, and to empower them (Luke 24:49; Ephesians 6:10). As for miracles, we all can agree it is the miraculous work of God's Spirit that transforms sinners (all of us) into the children of God who follow Christ. Should we not give praise to God when an abusive man repents with a broken heart and learns to love his family? Is it any less of a miracle when the Spirit transforms an egocentric young believer into a self-denying servant of God?

In chapter 5 of Galatians, Paul reasons that we should let the Spirit be the source of power and understanding we need for daily living. We should let the Spirit take the lead in all of our daily challenges. This means we are continually in prayerful contact with the Spirit, and we trust His power and faithfulness to bring Christ's lordship to bear on every aspect of our lives. Following the Spirit does mean seeking His leadership daily, but it is first about gratefully trusting the fact that the Spirit *is* leading.

Paul continues by saying that the flesh only produces immorality, hatred, fits of rage, contention, envy, selfishness, and all things that result from putting personal satisfaction above everything else (vv. 19–21). Then he lists the fruit of the Spirit as love, joy, peace, longsuffering, kindness, goodness, faithfulness, gentleness, and self-control (vv. 22–23).

Learning to yield to the Spirit is a process.

Jesus taught in a parable that we are like soil: if we surrender our flesh—our natural responses—to the Spirit of God (Matthew 13:3–9; Luke 8:4–8), we become good soil in which the seed of life can produce the peaceable fruit of the Spirit. If we don't yield to the Spirit, the seed of life doesn't root into our souls, which need transforming (mind, emotions, will, and so forth). Our flesh is then left to produce the fruits of our sin nature.

Notes from Benny's Journal
"LEARNING TO YIELD"

We must recognize that learning to yield to the Spirit is a process.

Many times during my own learning process, I have reacted to situations in my flesh. I responded out of my fears, personal wants, or an offended attitude. Nothing good ever came out of these times, but it is a learning process.

THE SPIRIT OF GOD IS TRUSTWORTHY. When we submit our will to the Spirit:

- God will, in time, make us trustworthy in the eyes of our children.
- we learn to be guided by the Holy Spirit, who will deliver us from the anxieties of raising children;
- God will pour His life into us, and we, in turn, will give life to our children instead of draining life out of them;
- the Spirit will teach us to practice willing submission to His leadership, and our children will follow us as we follow Him; and
- the Spirit will teach us to give generously and without fear. Our children will become compassionate by our example. They will see the trustworthiness of God as He provides for others through us.

THE HOLY SPIRIT PRODUCES DISCIPLES. You want your children to learn to hear the voice of God and follow the Spirit of God on their own. As they grow older, there will be less and less time when you will be available to them. But the Holy Spirit, living in them, will always be present to teach and guide your children in every situation and circumstance in which they find themselves.

It's no surprise that Jesus told Nicodemus that there are two kinds of birth, and that he must be born of the Spirit in order to live in God's kingdom (John 3:7). The Spirit points to Christ and says to us, "This is who you are made to be like." The Spirit empowered Jesus to see the kingdom of God as He lived in a broken world. And the Spirit will empower us to follow Jesus as He followed the Father. All we need to do is *listen*, and *follow* where He leads us. Ultimately, by listening and following, our journey will lead us to wisdom.

God Leads Supernaturally by Wisdom

At the beginning of this section, we looked at the story of the prodigal son. Why didn't the father of the prodigal say things like, "I told you you'd be back. I knew you were going to blow it. What did you do with the money?"

The Spirit will empower us to follow Jesus as He followed the Father.

The answer is because the prodigal son's father, like God, preferred to restore and not condemn his son. God wants us to be healed and restored before we are corrected. Similarly, this father had supernatural wisdom about how to encourage his son to become Godlike. The father didn't concern himself with what the son had done wrong. He didn't see himself or his son as a failure. The father chose only to see what his son *could* be. What the prodigal son did was wrong, but it wasn't failure.

Notes from Benny's Journal
"LEARNING TO WALK"

God is a perfect, loving heavenly Father. A great example of Godlike love is how a parent delights in watching her child learn to walk. The child tries to take a step but falls. Then, he takes his first successful step and falls again. He eventually takes two steps, then three, and keeps learning and falling. But exactly how many times does that child fall before he learns to walk? If we kept count, it could be hundreds or maybe thousands.

The focus of a loving parent is not on how many times his child falls but on the fact that his child is learning to walk. The parent delights in it. God is a delighted Father who continually picks us up, no matter how many times we fall, if we are truly trying to walk in His steps. Aren't we glad He doesn't keep count? God is not concerned about

how many times we fail, thanks to Christ and the cross. God's focus is that we will even-
tually become like Him.

When we refuse to learn from our mistakes, that is failure. Sin is more than wrongful thoughts and deeds; it's not reaching our God-designed destiny.

Just like the prodigal son's father, God says He forgets our sins but never forgets who we are becoming. The Bible says He even carves our names into His hand (Isaiah 49:16). God sees His children according to what He desires them to be. Is that how we see our children? Do we measure them by rights and wrongs? Dos and don'ts? Or do we teach them right and wrong convinced that they are becoming people of the right, no matter what they do along the way?

Being a parent like the prodigal son's father (or like God) means we have a stubborn, unfailing vision of what our children can become. This revelation will open the door to God's wisdom as we work through the struggle of daily living.

In the Book of James, we find insight about *asking* for wisdom (1:5–8). God's Holy Spirit will give us His wisdom if we ask, and He doesn't limit how many times we can ask. It's not like getting three wishes; He gives abundantly and doesn't get frustrated with us when we keep coming back. We must learn His voice, and we just have to trust that what He is telling us is the right thing to do. James says that if we keep second-guessing God, we will always be guessing and not following.

Just as Jesus explained to Nicodemus that there are two kinds of births, James also tells us there are two kinds of wisdom:

But if you have bitter jealousy and selfish ambition in your heart, do not
be arrogant and so lie against the truth. This wisdom is not that which
comes down from above, but is earthly, natural, demonic. For where jealousy
and selfish ambition exist, there is disorder and every evil thing. But the
wisdom from above is first pure, then peaceable, gentle, reasonable, full of

mercy and good fruits, unwavering, without hypocrisy. And the seed whose fruit is righteousness is sown in peace by those who make peace. James 3:14–18 (NASB)

James says there is a wisdom that comes from this world—but we live in a fallen world that is mostly built on lies and self-interest. That's why there is so much confusion and evil in the world. James is trying to tell us that Satan appeals to our flesh by promoting self-interest and greed for pleasure. It's so easy to let these things lead us because they are part of our fallen nature. But they don't bring peace. No matter how much we give to our flesh, we won't be satisfied.

If the world were built on this wisdom, peace would cover it instead of violence and fear.

James says there is also wisdom from heaven. People who live by this wisdom don't seek their own satisfaction first; they seek peace and mercy above all other things—even at their own expense. And the more we live by this wisdom of mercy and peace, the more this wisdom is planted in others. If the world were built on this wisdom, peace would cover it instead of violence and fear.

Just as we must move from physical birth to spiritual birth, remember that we must also grow up spiritually. We must replace the natural wisdom we use to protect our own interests with trust in God's supernatural wisdom of justice, mercy, and peace. We must be willing to let go of our agendas and personal ambitions. Parents definitely need to think clearly and act confidently. But they must also be able to follow the tender leading of the Spirit with a listening heart. Again, this requires the humility that comes with spiritual maturity.

- The natural parent who is driven by the flesh asks, "What's in it for me? How can I make sure I get what I want too?"
- The supernatural parent who is driven by God's wisdom asks,

"How is the Spirit leading me now? How does this bring glory to God?"

The prophet Micah tells us what God expects of us:

He has shown you, O man, what is good; And what does the LORD require of you But to do justly, To love mercy, And to walk humbly with your God. Micah 6:8 (NKJV)

The perfect fulfillment of this calling is love—God's love. There are five words used in New Testament Greek that are translated "love." Only one word—*agape*—is used to describe God's love. This love is the only kind in which there is no self-interest. No personal benefit is being sought when someone *loves like God does*, and this is the love that fulfills everything God requires of us.

For Review, Teaching, or Discussion

1. Briefly describe the difference between natural and supernatural living and parenting.

2. What is the certain result of spiritual maturity?

3. In the story of the prodigal son's father, what shows us God's fatherly love?

4. From God's perspective, what is a failed life?

5. What should be the guiding vision we have of our children?

6. What should we teach our children about God's biblical requirement of them?

7. How do rules and relationship play together, especially in regard to parenting?

chapter three

following a well-traveled road
how do I learn to lead my children?

A VIEW OF THE ROAD AHEAD:

- *Remembering the learning process*
- *Modeling leadership by attraction*
- *Learning seven principles of Godlike leadership*

There are three interesting facts to remember about the learning process:

1. You forget what you hear.
2. You remember what you see.
3. You understand what you experience.

I agree with these points, as I believe the best way to teach something is to model it. The ministry of Jesus and His teaching about leadership were revolutionary examples of this idea because He taught us that successful Godlike leadership is not a force of *compulsion*, but a force of *attraction*.

True Leadership: a Force of Attraction

Jesus says the greatest among us should be the servant of all (Matthew 23:11), and He proved it with His own life when He washed His disciples' feet. Ultimately, He proved it when He died for the sins of the world.

Leaders after God's own heart don't need to dominate others into submission. Instead, followers are drawn to them because of their humble devotion to something greater than themselves. Just look at the apostle Paul—his greatness as the leader of the gentile church wasn't in his preaching ability, his writings, or even the miracles he performed in Christ's name. Paul succeeded as a leader because he humbly followed Christ, and he attracted followers with his passion to that submission. In Philippians 1:21, Paul says, *"For to me, to live is Christ, and to die is gain"* (NKJV). So it's clear that Christ led His disciples to the Father from a heart of humble submission, and they followed in kind.

> *The best way to teach something is to model it.*

I understand that type of leadership; my parents pointed me to Christ in this way. And when you experience good parenting every day of your childhood and into your adult life, it becomes a part of you. It becomes a valuable resource for your own journey as a parent.

My Role Models

There were seven specific ways my parents were models of Godlike leadership to me; how they discipled me, loved me, disciplined me, and inspired me to follow the One they follow. Now don't get me wrong! Let me make it clear that my childhood home was not the portal of heaven, where angels sang and everything shined a light on God. My parents were very human, with real human weaknesses. I inherited some of their weaknesses, and I claim most of them as my own sinful nature. Therefore, my children didn't grow up at the portal of heaven either. Just go back and read the Foreword of this book. It was written by my mom and my wife, both of whom talk about their experiences in partnership with their husbands; and by my kids, who relate what it was like growing up in our home.

I want to honor my parents here, though, for how they raised me—not because they were perfect, but because they were full of love, grace, and mercy. In charting their course as parents, my mom and dad set standards that reached for the holiness of Jesus and applied the restoring grace of Jesus to all shortcomings, including their own. And despite their shortcomings, my parents were products of Godlike leadership in their homes. Their parents taught them wisely, and this prepared them to walk their children through the same legacy they were given. My parents didn't *force* me to this walk—they *attracted* me to it with the seven principles established as the climate of our home. I strive to walk in these principles because I want to continue the legacy. I offer these principles to you now, as they are perfect examples of what I've learned about leading by attraction.

Seven Ways My Parents Discipled Me

Principle #1: My parents loved each other and their children with abandon.

THEY LOVED UNASHAMEDLY. As I said in the previous chapter, the greatest gift parents can give to their children is to love each other. My parents showed affection to each other and to their children, openly and often ridiculously hugging, kissing, and laughing with each other, without holding back—even when they were in public. What seemed mushy and goofy to us as children became the foundation and expectation for a loving and secure future.

THEY LOVED TRUSTINGLY. I never heard my parents argue—although they must have had a few arguments—but if they did, it was in private. I'm convinced they chose to disagree in a way that built trust, rather than destruction, into their commitment to each other.

THEY LOVED HONESTLY. I experienced my parents' love in a home that was full of acceptance and availability. I was never rejected and never had to cautiously pick a good moment to approach them about something serious. Their love led to sacrifices of personal wants and produced an environment of personal value for each of their children.

THEY LOVED SACRIFICIALLY. My parents spent valuable time with each other and with their children. When my brother, sisters, and I were little, my parents were always getting down on the floor to play with us, never standing by passively or uninvolved. I don't remember my dad or mom ever missing a game I played, even if they had to drive through the night in order to be at work the next morning. Dad spent hours with me, throwing baseballs and rebounding basketballs to help me perfect my shooting. When it was raining or snowing, dad was up at five in the morning, helping me deliver my paper route before my school day and his work day began. Dad instilled in me a work ethic that has paid off a hundredfold in my life. He taught me the lessons of love and devotion on my journey through life. These things can't become part of you though lectures or Sunday school lessons.

THEY LOVED PATIENTLY. My parents' patient love gave them restraint when they had to discipline me. My dad wasn't afraid to punish me when I needed it, but neither he nor my mom ever punished their children when they were angry. We were sent to our rooms to let things cool off, and then we were punished. I don't think my dad ever read a book on parenting or discipline, but when I look back on how he handled discipline and punishment I realize he could have written one. His patient approach to discipline must have been passed down from his parents.

Notes from Benny's Journal
"A LESSON ON DISRESPECTFUL WORDS"

*There was one moment in my childhood that caused an exception to my dad's usual unprovokable nature. One day I was angry at my mom for not letting me have my way, and I told her I hated her. That was a **big** mistake! In our home, Mom was the queen and no one insulted Dad's queen at any time—especially in front of him. He heard what I said, and the next thing I remember is lying on the floor, looking up at my crying mother and angry dad standing over me. He said, "Don't ever say that to your mother again." And I didn't.*

I've never apologized so quickly or fervently as I did that moment. As much as my dad sacrificed to love his children, that day he taught me that the core of a home is a husband and wife; that although he would valiantly defend his children, marriage comes first and before any other relationship.

I see so many children talk back to their mothers with no accountability to their fathers. Allowing a child to disrespect or dishonor his mother is a big mistake on the part of a father. A habit of disrespectful back talk can be prevented if it is dealt with when a child is young.

I remember reading an article by Billy Graham that said the best way to solve big problems is while they're still little problems. My dad's belt, some occasional soap in the mouth, and consistent loving discipline were great deterrents to disrespectful words.

THEY LOVED JOYFULLY. Laughter was a much larger part of our home environment than discipline. Our parents taught us to laugh together, even when life was especially difficult. We'd pass the time in the car on road trips by singing, playing games, and telling jokes. Unlike many families today, we shared most of our lives together, and we enjoyed it. Our whole family sang in the church choir. When my family missed church, the choir didn't sound the same. My family life was so much fun and there was so much affection that friends loved to be at my house.

THEY LOVED PURELY AND SIMPLY. The purity and power of my parents' love overshadowed the fact that we didn't have much in the way of material things. We were actually quite poor at times, but I didn't know it. When I was little, mom and dad would watch their four children eat dinner, but they wouldn't be eating. I wondered how I could be so famished while they didn't seem to be hungry. As I got older, I realized they were making sure their children got all they needed, and then if there was anything left, they would eat. Now that's love!

Principle #2: My parents loved all people equally.

I remember how my parents treated people outside our family. It didn't matter if they were employees or employers; regular customers or strangers; white, black, Southern, Northern, or foreign. Nothing affected their common love, gracious attitude, and merciful acts toward people. Nothing ever provoked them to condemn or to be critical—even though, like everyone, they had many opportunities to do so. Like Christ, they simply chose not to use words to harm anyone. In leading their children to follow Christ's example of love for others, they set the bar high indeed.

Notes from Benny's Journal
"NO RACIAL BOUNDARIES"

My first year of high school was the year public schools were lawfully integrated. I grew up in the middle of the racial unrest of the 1950s and '60s in East Tennessee, but my parents never planted a prejudicial thought in my mind. All people were equally valuable to God and equally welcome in our lives and our home. I was able to hang out with close friends who were black during a time when that was very offensive to most people—white and black.

April 4, 1968, was my eighteenth birthday, and half the kids at my party were black. Unfortunately, news came in the middle of the party that Martin Luther King, Jr. had been murdered. The party ended, but my relationships with black friends didn't. In the midst of that tragic time when there were riots in my high school, my friendships, and I personally, benefited from the influence of my parents and others who accepted all people as equal.

That same year, I entered my freshman year in college on a basketball scholarship. I was asked by the coach to room with the first black athlete our school had ever recruited. That was obviously no problem for me. In fact, it became quite a novelty because Joe was six foot nine and very black; I was five foot nine and very white. His last name was Gaines; mine was Proffitt. We became the captains of the basketball team, and the local newspapers had fun with our names throughout both our college careers.

Principle #3: They compassionately served people in need.

My parents' devotion to the love of God had a tremendous effect on their attitudes toward the world. It touched every encounter they had with people, mercifully and compassionately.

When my dad owned a service station, he often had to rescue people who were stranded with a broken-down car. He took good care of his customers, and even though some who were in distress expected him to take advantage of them, my dad never did.

There are people who love things and use people, and then there are those who love people and use things. My mom and dad were definitely the latter. I realize now we were probably considered poor. But I thought we were well off because we often gave clothes, food, or money to people in dire need. Frequently people stayed in our home overnight or for even longer periods of time. Some of the stranded customers from the service station who couldn't afford a hotel came home with my dad, and mom fed them dinner. Mom and dad showed their children that serving others and living out the selfless mercy of God was what the love of God was all about.

My parents also taught me to desire compassion before comfort and mercy before judgment. Occasionally, I'll see someone in need and feel troubled about whether to help them or not. It could be argued that in some cases it might be wiser to let someone struggle and work his way out of his mess, lest we end up encouraging a harmful, dependent lifestyle. But my

Desire compassion before comfort and mercy before judgment.

parents' actions taught me that when I have no clear direction, God would have me err on the side of mercy and generosity to all people in need. If people ever deceive me into helping them, I will answer to God for doing what seems right, and they must answer to God for their deceit.

We should try to hear God's voice of wisdom in all our interactions with people. The goal is always to bring glory to God by demonstrating His mercy. After all, every one of us is desperately in daily need of God's mercy.

Principle #4: They served the church and God's anointed people.

Our involvement as a family in a local church was not a schedule of church events; it was a way of life to which my mom and dad were committed. Dad was a deacon and Sunday school teacher in our church. My mom still teaches a Sunday school class, just like she has for the last fifty years. They both sang in the choir, and eventually our whole family did the same.

They also used our home as a place of ministry to serve others. Visiting preachers, missionaries, or other people in full-time ministry were often served meals in our home and supported with prayer and encouragement. Whenever something needed to be done in the church or for someone in the body of Christ, my parents were often the ones to see the need met.

My parents willingly served all people, but they regarded fellow believers as family. The dinner table conversations with these servants of God and their stories from around the world that told of God's faithfulness played a significant role in the development of my faith in Christ.

Through stories, I discovered that my grandparents were just like my parents. Many visiting preachers looked forward to the home-cooked meals and genuine hospitality of my parents because they had also enjoyed such ministry from my grandparents. It's a great investment in your children's lives to have them partner with you in providing hospitality to people who have such an adventurous commitment to ministry and missions. Marilou and I made an effort to do this, and my children have, at times, expressed the influence it had upon them.

As Christians, we—not church buildings—are the Church. Unfortunately, many people think going to a church is enough to make them followers of Christ. My parents lived as members of the true Church—the body of Christ. Their lives were the temple of a very present God, who was the honored guest.

Principle #5: They emphasized family prayer and following God's Word.

Mom or dad, usually both, would regularly sit down with their children and lead us in family devotions and prayer. God's Word was the basis for all celebration, conflict resolution, and standard for acceptable behavior. It wasn't a forced, legalistic practice; it was just a natural part of our daily routine throughout our lives. Every day—usually before bed— Mom and Dad would read the Bible and pray alone and together. This is why they were so united and loving to each other throughout their marriage.

Hearing and applying the Word of God was so much at the center of our lives, it never occurred to me until I was grown that there were people who didn't live that way. I wasn't raised to seek the opinions of men or man's interpretations of God's Word. I was raised on the chapter and verse in God's Word. Oftentimes, I would have a question or a problem, and my mom or dad would show me a verse from the Bible that revealed the truth to me. Every decision my parents made could be traced directly back to the truth in God's Word.

All things in my parents' lives had their meaning and purpose in the joy of their fellowship with God. Prayer covered everything. We prayed at the table over meals, in the living room with visitors and people in need, when we went to bed, and often when we came together in the morning. I also remember, in difficult times, overhearing soft-spoken, tearful conversations about not having enough money to pay the bills and what must be done to simply survive. Because my parents emphasized living by prayer and the truth of God's Word, those are what continue to govern my life today; they became a natural part of me, which in turn shaped me as a parent.

Principle #6: They openly confessed their faith in Jesus Christ.

Talking about Jesus was a natural part of my parents' life. My mother had the gifts to communicate, teach, and tell stories. My dad was a quieter person, but he spoke with kindness and wisdom. Mom always talked to us about how people needed Jesus and how we should tell others about Him. She was the bold witness, naturally finding ways to bring Christ into every conversation, pointing people to His love, and sharing the message of salvation. Dad was not as overt as Mom, but he often shared with his children and many others his love for and commitment to Christ. Throughout my life, I have encountered people who have shared with me how my parents encouraged them to put their faith in Christ.

My parents filled their daily lives with conversations about faith in Christ, and their faith dominated every decision about their direction in life.

Principle #7: They reflected the character of Jesus in words and deeds.

Humans usually develop the skill of adjusting their personalities and approaches to different people according to various situations. We're driven by our sin nature to protect ourselves and gain advantage where we can by changing like chameleons to suit our environment. But we don't think of Jesus as being that way. We think of Him as the same recognizable person, whether He was eating with His disciples or whipping thieves out of the temple. He didn't care about protecting Himself or pressing His advantage. He was free to be who He was in all situations—an attractive quality His disciples eventually acquired and passed on to their followers.

It was important for me to overhear my youngest son, Joey, say, "My dad is always the same wherever he is," because that was exactly how I felt about my parents. It didn't matter if they were at home, at church, at work, or at a social occasion; they were the same people because they were followers of Christ. They reflected His character and learned to be the same faithful people in every relationship, responsibility, challenge, and circumstance. I never heard a profane word nor gossip or bad talk about anyone come out of their mouths. They only talked about others to express appreciation for them or to discuss how to help them. Wouldn't this be a great legacy for you to leave your children, grandchildren, and great-grandchildren?

My parents weren't perfect. They weren't born Godlike people. They became like Christ by following Him as closely as they could throughout their lives. They so desired to reflect the character of Jesus in all they did, it's hard to remember their flaws. They were selfless and humble, thinking of others and serving every day, and, at the same time, they were firmly committed to the truth of God's Word. Whether they were teaching, working, playing, or disciplining us, they were motivated by sacrificial love.

Finishing Well, Regardless . . .

Every successful parent I know has some kind of Godlike leadership in his or her life. If your parents aren't your model of Godlike parenting, please pray that God will put someone with those leadership qualities in your path so you can submit yourself to learning from them. It's so important for you to learn and trust the dynamic of following those who have gone before you.

If your upbringing or past parenting styles have been less than idyllic, there is still a way you can be remembered as a success. The fact is, you didn't choose your parents, and you can't undo all their mistakes; but you can choose how you finish *your* life. Make choices today that will change the course of past failures that have your family trapped in generational sin. Respond to the call of Christ, ask forgiveness for the wounds you've caused others, and let Him heal your wounds. He will restore you to the life He desires for you—a life of walking in humble submission, seeking first His kingdom, and trusting only in His strength and righteousness instead of your own.

In God's eyes, success isn't having a perfect record, not as we define perfection. Success is finishing well.

In God's eyes, success isn't having a perfect record, not as we define perfection. Success is finishing well. We fail when we don't become the people God intends us to be.

Principles to Live By

1. Love each other and your children with abandon (1 Corinthians 13).
2. Love all people equally (Galatians 5:14).
3. Compassionately serve people in need (Matthew 25:34–40).
4. Serve the church and God's anointed people (1 Corinthians 12:24–26; Ephesians 4:15–16).
5. Emphasize family prayer and following God's Word (Psalms 42:1; Matthew 7:21–25; Luke 9:23–24; John 14:15–17).
6. Openly confess your faith in Jesus Christ (Psalms 40:16, 107:2; Matthew 10:32–33; Romans 1:16).
7. Let your words and deeds reflect the character of Jesus (2 Corinthians 5:17; 1 Peter 2:21; 1 John 2:3–6).

check
point

Set aside time, in quality *and* quantity, to do these things with your spouse and children:

1. Write down the existing family principles that are characteristic of your home.

2. Make a list of things (attitudes or actions) that need to change in your home.

3. Sit down with your family and discuss the lists.
4. Pray with your family, asking God to forgive past failures and lead

your family into the future.

5. Then, rewrite your family principles, according to the priorities God would have you set for your family.

6. Present the new principles to your family for approval.

7. Make a copy of the new principles for each family member and post a nicely framed copy somewhere in your home.

8. Make a list of Godlike examples of parents you know, and ask these people to be your partners and mentors in parenting. If you don't know anyone who could mentor you, pray that God will help you find someone.

chapter four

the battle plan

how can I win the battle against the enemy of my soul?

A VIEW OF THE ROAD AHEAD:
- *Catching a vision of the battle plan*
- *Making battle preparations*
- *Engaging the enemy in battle*
- *Renewing our spiritual strength*

Learning to listen to and follow the Spirit and pursuing the example of godly leadership are not like flipping on a switch. The Christian life is a constant battle; it will never be over until Christ returns and banishes the enemies of our souls. For now, victory in this battle is constantly won or lost.

The great thing about our call to battle is that the end of each day can be celebrated for the day's victories. And every day can be victorious if we kneel in submission to the Spirit, stand firm on the truth He speaks to us, and charge boldly against the enemy with the strength He gives us. As we follow our Commander into battle, we can lead our children to victory in their own lives.

When an army plans to go against an enemy, there are three main phases of operation that must be at work at all times. The three-part battle for supernatural living, and thus supernatural parenting, is a strategy involving the same three phases of operation:

- Preparation (Putting on the Armor of God)
- Execution (Engaging the Enemy)
- Support (Renewing Our Spiritual Life)

We must engage in the battle between our flesh and our spirit. So, first we are going to learn how God calls us to prepare and equip ourselves before we go into battle. Then, we will learn how to engage the enemy with power as God leads us. Finally, we need to be continually resupplied in order to fight without growing weary, so we'll see how we receive strengthening life support from God in order to continue to win spiritual victories in our lives and our children's lives.

Preparation

The first phase of battle is preparation, which involves training and equipping. An army needs to count the cost of taking a city and be prepared for it (Luke 14:28-31).

The battle begins when we are faced with a situation that requires our response. Life is a constant flow of questions and answers, conflict and resolution, challenge and our response.

Our first response to challenges should be another question that we, perhaps prayerfully, ask ourselves: *Am I being ruled by my flesh right now, or am I dying to myself and being led by God's Spirit?*

Our flesh is the part of our nature that fights to stay in first place; it's like a two-year-old, living inside of us, not thinking, feeling, or believing in anything except fulfilling what it wants. Our goal in learning to walk in the Spirit is to subdue our spoiled flesh. Even Paul moaned about his flesh interfering with his desire to follow Christ (see Romans 7:15). Paul could be called the most self-abandoned Christian in history, yet in his letter to the Romans he describes the battle between the flesh and the spirit. He concludes in Romans 8:2 that his only hope is that the law of the Spirit of life in Christ Jesus has made him free from the law of sin and death. He continues by saying:

That the righteous requirement of the law might be fulfilled in us who do not walk according to the flesh but according to the Spirit. For those who live according to the flesh set their minds on the things of the flesh, but those who live according to the Spirit, the things of the Spirit. For to be carnally minded is death, but to be spiritually minded is life and peace. Romans 8:4-6 (NKJV)

Paul shows us that we haven't been separated from our flesh, but in Christ we have been set free from domination by it. We choose each day to live either according to the Spirit's leading or to the leading of our flesh. The Spirit gives us life; the flesh is dying so it can only give death.

Arm Yourself

Take up the whole armor of God, that you may be able to withstand in the evil day, and having done all, to stand. Stand therefore, having girded your waist with truth, having put on the breastplate of righteousness, and having shod your feet with the preparation of the gospel of peace; above all, taking the shield of faith with which you will be able to quench all the fiery darts of the wicked one. And take the helmet of salvation, and the sword of the Spirit, which is the word of God. Ephesians 6:13-17 (NKJV)

Everything God is doing in your life, Satan will try to kill. What God gives you, Satan will try to steal. What God is building in you, Satan will try to destroy (John 10:10). You shouldn't get ready for battle

You shouldn't get ready for battle because it might come; you must get ready for battle because it surely will come.

because it *might* come; you must get ready for battle because it surely *will* come.

Before you go into battle you must have the right armor. Yours is a spiritual battle (Ephesians 6:12), and spiritual war requires spiritual weapons provided by God.

THE CONVICTION OF TRUTH. The first piece of armor you need is the firm support of *truth*. In order for God's truth to become a weapon you can use, you need two things:

1. You must know in your innermost being that what God says is true.
2. You must put your trust in what He says above all other resources.

Resting in God's truth is where your core strength is, which is why Paul says it girds your waist. Mountain climbers will tell you that core strength (abdomen, hips, and lower back) are more important to them than arm or leg strength.

RIGHTEOUSNESS. The *breastplate of righteousness* has to do with whose righteousness it is that protects your heart from the accusations of the enemy. There is no condemnation for those who protect their hearts with the breastplate of Christ's righteousness (Romans 8:1).

Your own righteousness is easily broken by the cutting blows of the enemy, but putting your trust in Christ's righteousness will give you confidence to stand against your accuser and prevent you from trying to face him alone.

PEACE. With your feet shod (covered) with the *gospel of peace*, you are able to run with confidence. You know the curse upon the earth no longer touches your feet or keeps you in bondage to the law of sin and death. In fact, the gospel declares that your spirit is holy in Christ, and you are being purified in your mind and heart because all things are now being used for your good (Romans 8:28).

FAITH. If you are armed well with the weapons mentioned above, Satan will know that he can't bring you under the curse, make you reject

God's truth, or cause you to doubt the value of Christ's righteousness. He will, however, try to plant various fears of the world and self-doubt into your soul.

Your defense must not be to trust in your own strength against the uncertainties in life or threats from the world. Your confession of trust in Christ's strength is your *shield of faith* against the fiery darts of fear and self-doubt. With faith in Christ's strength in front of you, the enemy's lies cannot reach you.

ASSURANCE OF SALVATION. The *helmet of salvation* refers to your anointing in the Spirit. In the old covenant with Israel, ceremonial anointing with oil was always done on the head. The Old Testament often refers to the anointed head of the deliverer. It is your anointing in the Spirit that gives you the inner assurance of your salvation.

One of Satan's attacks is the way he tries to use your sins or incidental failures to provoke doubt about your salvation. You know Christ is *the* Deliverer, but Satan likes to confuse your mind with doubts that Christ is *your* Deliverer. Have you ever considered the parable Jesus taught about the wheat and the tares (Matthew 13:24–30)? In a discouraged moment did you think you must be a tare instead of wheat? Those discouraged thoughts come from the enemy. He is whispering to you, "You know the tares look just like wheat, but they are worthless like you."

You must reject these lies and realize that you couldn't even be troubled by such thoughts unless you were already a redeemed child of God. Firmly strap the helmet of salvation on because you didn't earn it—it was given to you. You not only *can* wear it freely, you *must* wear it freely in order to honor the price Jesus paid to give it to you.

THE WORD OF GOD. Finally, you must arm yourself with the *sword of God's Word*. Remember that girding your waist with truth was about making yourself ready to confess from your heart God's truth. With confidence in God's truth and all the other armor, you have all the defense you need against the enemy of your soul. A sword is an offensive weapon. It is the one thing with which you can strike at your enemy. But it is also the last piece of armor you take up before you do battle.

You must be prepared by taking on the whole armor of God before you try to strike with the sword. Without conviction of truth, confidence in the cross, certainty of your deliverance from the curse, faith in God's strength, and assurance of your salvation, swinging the sword around will win few if any battles. An army of believers armed with God's Word and totally surrendered confidence in Him is like a weapon of mass destruction against the enemy's kingdom.

Begin your preparation for battle by putting on the whole armor of God. Then you will be ready to execute God's battle plan and destroy the enemy's fortresses (2 Corinthians 10:4).

Execution

The second phase of battle is execution, whereas the army confidently engages the enemy offensively or defensively (Ephesians 6:10). Sometimes we will be holding our ground, and other times we'll be taking ground. The following are strategies and resources our General has given us with which to fight well.

Pray for Power

The earnest (heartfelt, continued) prayer of a righteous man makes tremendous power available [dynamic in its working]. James 5:16 (AMP)

There are many aspects to prayer, including adoration, confession, intercession, and supplication. As a whole, though, all prayer follows the same call and response motion that all of life—especially spiritual life—entails. It is speaking and listening, inhaling and exhaling. Some say that since we have two ears and one mouth we should listen twice as much as we speak. In our prayer to God, we should probably listen at least ten times as much as we speak.

We also have the ability to wield much power in battle by speaking to God directly or by confessing His truth allowed in a prayerful and faith-empowered way. Fervent prayer with power is not just imploring

God intensely to do something we want Him to do. The fervent prayer of a righteous man is one that agrees with what God says and then confesses it with all his heart, soul, mind, and strength.

For our prayers to have power, they must be pure and without contradiction in our lives. For instance, when we pray the Lord's Prayer we are making a covenant with the Lord to link our forgiveness with our forgiving. When we take communion in church, we are stating before God and the whole church body that we are trusting in the shed blood and broken body of Jesus alone for our redemption from sin and death; we are also declaring this whenever we call ourselves followers of Christ with our cross necklaces and fish bumper stickers.

The fervent prayer of a righteous man is one that agrees with what God says and then confesses it with all his heart, soul, mind, and strength.

If we thought carefully about the things we do, we might realize we are making more serious statements than we know. The real question is this: are we making honest declarations of truth that we live by and rejecting all contradictions every day, or are we being double-minded by declaring truth one day and contradicting ourselves the next?

In the Old Covenant, the prophets were unique among men because they heard directly from God, but they also had the ear of God. God even relented from what He intended sometimes after the fervent prayers of prophets like Moses and Amos. What we need to recognize about the prophets is that they were committed to what God said, even if it threatened their lives to report it to the people. They accepted what God said as their own truth, even when they didn't like it, and they resisted all claims that contradicted God.

Many Christians will pray with great faith in God's deliverance or healing and even pray with surrender to His will instead of theirs. But then they lose heart and stop praying when God seems slow in answering or when the answer isn't easy enough. To have power in prayer you need to do two things:

1. Say the same things God says.
2. Say them as though there are no other options.

For instance, if you want your children to accept their need for forgiveness and trust in the redemption available through Christ, then you already want what God wants. Ask God for this miracle, and keep asking without doubting that God will deliver it. But then you must parent your children as though you truly believe they belong to God and that you answer to Him for how you raise them. Don't worry about mistakes and setbacks. Concern yourself only with making sure your prayers and declarations before God are honest and true from your heart. This is called single-mindedness; it's when you are one mind with God and your life shows it (Hebrews 10:23).

> You must parent your children as though you truly believe they belong to God.

With the whole armor of God and a surrendered, single-minded commitment to what God says, you can pray with power that comes from righteousness far greater than that of the prophets. You can take this weapon of fervent prayer and engage the enemy, expecting victory.

Plan to Resist

> *Yet in all these things we are more than conquerors through Him who loved us.* Romans 8:37 (NKJV)

Satan does flee when we resist with humble trust and dependence on Go̶ presence, but he never gives up. He has many tactics we can't
ɔ from using against us.
ʔple of our enemy's craftiness is in his use of flattery. If he
ɘ to lead us into sin or a self-destructive lifestyle, he will

influence us to become proud of our spiritual strength. We can become self-congratulating and confident in our ability to make the enemy flee. In short, he tries to flatter us away from our source of strength. We become distracted from our continual attitude of prayer and dependence on the Spirit.

Satan may also tempt us to become afraid and to doubt God's nearness when someone we care about is hurt or dies. He will attack either our confidence in God's trustworthiness or our assurance about our position in Christ.

We must stay close to the source of our strength. But we must also be prepared at all times to recognize the enemy's work in our hearts and be ready to resist with the whole armor of God. The battle will be more difficult for us if we are always taken by surprise—if we are always on the defensive. Being ready to resist at all times so the enemy never gains ground in our lives is an offensive strategy. Again, the enemy flees when we stand against him with our trust in the Lordship of Christ, but he won't be destroyed by it until his final judgment. He will always come back, so we must plan to resist him. We must be ready to recognize Satan's attacks and respond instantly with knowledge of God's Word, certainty of its truth, and stubborn confidence in its power to repel the enemy's deceptions.

Perform True Righteousness

> For we are His workmanship, created in Christ Jesus for good works, which God prepared beforehand that we should walk in them. Ephesians 2:10 (NKJV)

We are the righteousness of God in Christ (2 Corinthians 5:21). As Christians we have what theologians call a *foreign righteousness*. Our right standing before God has nothing to do with our worthiness. It comes from the worthiness of someone else—Jesus. But the Bible also tells us that we should *pursue* righteousness.

Righteousness has two sides just like a coin; besides our position of righteousness in Christ, righteousness has to do with our faith-centered works as well. One of the evidences of spiritual maturity is choosing to do the right thing when we are faced with choices. The right thing is always what honors God and promotes mercy as well as justice. We are doing the right thing when we choose justice over self-interest. We are doing right with our mercy and charity toward others in the love of God.

We don't tell our children to be righteous because that would just sound funny to them. We tell them to do the right thing. And if we have done a good job countering our culture's decaying view of right and wrong, they will understand what we mean. As we've already learned, you will best disciple your children to replace the world's ways with God's ways if you perform them yourself.

Performing true righteousness is a battle strategy in two ways. First, committing in your heart to do the right thing at all times, even if you're sometimes unsure what the right thing is, keeps you facing in God's direction and better prepared to recognize the enemy's deceptions. Second, good works are rewarded by God; they are personally fulfilling and they tend to open doors of opportunity for greater works. The more filled our lives are with good works, the less vulnerable we are to Satan's attacks on our idleness.

God has already prepared good works for you to do through His strength. Sometimes they will be works of mercy towards others. Other times they will be opportunities for you to experience victory over hardship, temptation, or conflict. But the enemy will try to deceive or flatter you again, so you must be ready to resist. You must recognize that the works of your own righteousness are not the good works of Christ in you (Isaiah 64:6; Titus 3:5). Works of true righteousness are not self-promoting but are performed through the power of faith in Christ and in response to the leading of God's Spirit (Ephesians 2:10).

Proclaim the Truth

> *For with the heart one believes unto righteousness, and with the mouth confession is made unto salvation.* Romans 10:10 (NKJV)

If we are being diligent to prepare ourselves with knowledge and understanding of God's Word, then we are taking up the sword of the Spirit. Then we can use God's Word as a weapon against our enemy by proclaiming it as our answer to anything that challenges our trust in God (2 Corinthians 10:4-5). This is how we use God's truth as an offensive weapon. When we know and accept the deliverance of Christ, we are made righteous in Him. But when we proclaim the truth of God's Word with our mouths, we are actively claiming the deliverance bought for us by Christ and counterattacking the enemy's position.

Jesus Himself is our example of proclaiming the truth in battle with the enemy. His answer to Satan's temptations, recorded in the Gospels, was to quote Scripture. He could have just ignored Satan, but He chose to fight with the sword of God's Word. His parents had no doubt obeyed God's command to fill their house with His Word (Deuteronomy 11:18-21). Jesus was even prepared, at the age of twelve, to wisely answer the temple priests. Our children can learn to wisely answer the world, the devil, and their flesh at a young age.

But we don't have to be able to quote the Scripture perfectly to make the enemy flee. It isn't just the words which the enemy fears. What terrifies him most is the fact that you know the words and can firmly stand by faith on what they mean. The power behind your confession of God's Word is the same as your power in prayer. Let's look at an example of proclaiming the truth offensively:

> *There is no fear in love; but perfect love casts out fear, because fear involves torment. But he who fears has not been made perfect in love. We love Him because He first loved us.* 1 John 4:18-19 (NKJV)

Just quoting this verse perfectly may not drive away fear and anxiety. The words of God are not magic tricks—they're truth. Standing on them confidently is what makes them powerful. To make the words powerful, they must be true in your own heart and life. It's not enough just to speak them. The book of Acts tells us how Jewish exorcists and the sons of Sceva failed and suffered when they tried to use the power of the Word against a demon when the Word wasn't in their hearts (Acts 19:11–16).

John shows us in 1 John 4 that before you can drive fear away you must be made perfect in love. John doesn't mean you must be a perfect person. John is talking about the content of your heart. After all, fear resides in the heart. Satan is only able to put it there when God's love is lacking. The fear must be driven out with God's perfect love. For that to happen, God's love must replace the selfish love in your heart. As long as you walk in God's love there is no place for fear to enter in. That's what being perfected in love means.

You know you have God's love in your heart if you feel broken-hearted for people—even enemies—who don't know Christ. You have God's perfect love if you can see pain in the heart of someone who is trying to hurt you. That doesn't stop you from protecting the innocent and defending justice. But your pursuit of justice is tempered by love instead of rage. That's when you can stand against fear truthfully—because you are being perfected in love. Then you can say to the devil, "God says I don't have to be afraid of anything because I know His love is in me. I know God's love, Devil. I don't just *believe*, I *know*."

You see, it is standing on what you *know* God has done in your life that reveals the deception of Satan and exposes his intention, leaving him powerless; it is not merely quoting God's Word. Satan doesn't exactly fear the Word of God; he quotes it all the time. He knows it better than any of us. It is our confident trust in God and His Word that Satan fears and hates. He is filled with fear and rage because he chose selfishly to reject God's authority, and he can never experience grace or be perfected in love.

But we can be. We can pursue God-like love in everything we do. And this introduces us to our last offensive battle strategy.

Pursue Love

Let all that *you* do *be done with love.* 1 Corinthians 16:14 (NKJV)

Love gets the last word in this part of the battle plan because love fulfills all of God's will. First Corinthians 13:13 says the greatest of the gifts from God is love. If you love God with all your heart, soul, mind, and strength and love others just as you would yourself, then you have all of God's law written on your heart. You will fulfill God's law not just out of discipline but out of your new heart.

The Spirit is bearing fruit in your heart, and you are building a new nature. This new nature is shaped by the presence of God's spirit of love. But we must continue to yield to the Spirit's presence in order to continue to grow in the Spirit.

Notes from Benny's Journal
"MOVE A LITTLE CLOSER"

You've probably heard the story of the old couple riding through town in their car with the old man at the wheel and his wife sitting on the passenger side. At a stoplight a young couple pulls up beside them and they are snuggled up very close together. The old woman sighs and says, "Oh, I miss the days we used to do that." The old man glances at his wife with a crooked smile saying, "Well honey, I'm not the one who moved." Within seconds the old couple was snuggling and being giddy like when they were younger. This is such a sweet story, but it really illustrates how we lose our hearts when we don't stay close to God.

King David drifted from obedience to God, and his solution was to cry out to Him to restore to him the joy of God's salvation (Psalm 51:12).

We fall away because it is we who move away and not God. We lose our first love like the people in the church at Ephesus (Revelation 2:4). We don't want our lamp to go out. We can only burn brightly with God's Spirit if we walk in His love. And we can only walk in God's love if we stay close to Him as our first love. Present yourself to God and pursue His love, not just as a battle strategy but as a gift of love to Him.

As you *put on the armor of God*, don't forget to put on God's love

> We can only walk in God's love if we stay close to Him as our first love.

(Colossians 3:14). *Pray* for the Holy Spirit to show you the mysteries of God's love and pray for the faith to walk in them. Fill your heart with the strength of God's love as you *plan to resist* the enemy's attack. *Do what is right* and do it because love compels you— not because you want something in return. *Proclaim the truth* about God's love and the trustworthiness of God's promises for those who walk in love. *Love* in spite of yourself, in spite of discomfort, and in spite of injustice. Love ridiculously; love radically. This is how God loves.

Support

The final phase of battle involves keeping supply lines open so the army can remain strong against its enemy. It's important to maintain continual support behind it (Philippians 4:19). In our mission to become supernatural parents, it is the same General going before us in battle who also keeps us strong and supplied in spirit. As you might discover, He does both of these things in similar ways.

As Christians we have flesh and we have spirit. In the battle between our flesh and our spirit, it is the one we feed that will win. The apostle Paul tells us if we sow to the flesh it will bring the only thing it can— death. But if we sow to the Spirit we will reap the life of the Spirit

> In the battle between our flesh and our spirit, it is the one we feed that will win.

(Galatians 6:7-8). We can focus our lives on opportunities to please our flesh, or we can give ourselves to the kingdom of God's Spirit to be strengthened by the Spirit. Our faith in the trustworthiness of God can become weak over time if we neglect our need for continual, regular nourishment and strengthening by the Spirit. We cannot grow from faith to faith (Romans 1:17) if we forget that we're in a battle and drift away from the life of the Spirit. Whatever is fed, our flesh or our spirit, will win the day.

So now we will learn how to trust God as the One who strengthens and renews us with His Spirit.

Our Supply Lines of Spiritual Strength

GOD STRENGTHENS US WITH THE LOVE OF THE FATHER. To accomplish His glorious plan for us, God didn't just give the best of what He had. God gave Himself. To give us spiritual life He gives of His own Spirit. It brings God much glory to give us His Spirit. But the Bible makes clear that love is what motivates Him (John 3:16).

So, for instance, when we stand on the truth that perfect love casts out fear, we understand that the love we are perfected in is God Himself. We can abide in that love the way children rest in the arms of their fathers. A little child trusts his or her father not just because of his strong arms but mostly because of his welcoming love. No one is stronger, more faithful, and more welcoming than God the Father!

Can there be any doubt that the love of the Father is a lifeline of strength for us? And how differently would we live if we deeply believed and trusted in the Father's unconditional love? Unconditional love is God's example to us of true fatherhood.

GOD STRENGTHENS US WITH ASSURANCE OF OUR SALVATION IN CHRIST. We've talked about putting on this assurance as armor. Where does this assurance come from? Our salvation is in Christ because it was the price paid by Jesus that purchased our forgiveness and the gift of God's Spirit. The first among many things the Spirit gives us is assurance of our position in Christ. It isn't a conviction of the mind; it's a deep-seated confidence in our hearts from the Holy Spirit that we are forgiven and now belong to God in Christ. We must be continually reassured of our acceptance in Christ through our yielding, intimate relationship with Him.

Jesus was born of the Holy Spirit. He walked His whole life in the Spirit. He heard from the Spirit and obeyed Him with confident faith. The faithfulness and faith of Jesus is His example to us of true Sonship. Jesus knew who He was as He walked by faith, just as the Spirit reassures us of who we are in Christ. We are called to walk as Jesus did.

GOD STRENGTHENS US BY LIVING IN US THROUGH THE HOLY SPIRIT. God brings the spiritually dead to life with His Spirit that is given to them by Jesus. It is the Holy Spirit that brings them to life with God's very presence living in them. If you are newborn in Christ, you are spiritually alive because God actually lives inside of you.

This is a mystery because the Scripture says God is present everywhere and isn't confined to temples. And yet the temple of Solomon was said to be the dwelling place of God. It was death for anyone but the high priest to enter the holiest place where the presence of God was. And now we not only have audience freely with God through Christ, we *are* the temple where God dwells.

Notes from Benny's Journal
"A NEW WAY TO PRAY"

*Realizing the truth of God's presence in me changed my prayer life forever. I used to lift my head and pray to God as if He were somewhere beyond the stars. Then one night I just felt God speaking to my spirit, saying, "You're praying in the wrong direction. I'm right here. I'm inside you. I see everything you see and more. I feel everything you feel. I understand you and your life better than you ever will. You are always in My presence because I am not just **with** you, I am **in** you."*

This experience was like a revelation for me because it changed my spiritual life. It wasn't that I didn't know about the indwelling of the Holy Spirit. But for the first time it was real and personal for me. I began to pray to the God who was in me and not a million miles away. I knew the Spirit was really with me and could hear every thought and concern that went through my mind. I knew He had compassion for my prayers and patient, fatherly correction for my sins. This is the power of the Spirit of God.

God is able to live in every believer. His power and life can flow to the world out of every believer who yields to Him. God is living in followers of Christ through His Spirit. Our enemy doesn't want us to have this revelation though. But it's all right there in God's Word (Romans 8:10; 2 Corinthians 1:22, 13:5; Ephesians 3:16; Colossians 1:27). The Spirit makes this truth come alive in our hearts and clear in our understanding. This is how God strengthens us through His Spirit (1 John 4:4).

GOD STRENGTHENS US BY WRITING HIS WORD ON OUR HEARTS. The apostle John tells us that Jesus is the Word made flesh (John 1:1, 14). We can't begin to understand the power of the Spirit's connection to the Word of God. And certainly, we could never learn all the wisdom of God even if it could all be written down. John said that the world couldn't hold the books that could be written about the life of Jesus alone (John 21:25). But we can read and grow to understand what He has chosen to reveal to us in the Bible.

The Bible is God's revealed truth to mankind. As we read and search it with a yielding heart, the Spirit that lives within us will open our understanding to it. He will then lead us to walk in all the light He gives us by presenting opportunities to do so. If we keep a yielding heart, the Spirit will strengthen us to walk in the revelation He gives us through our study of His Word.

GOD STRENGTHENS US THROUGH OUR SPIRIT-LED PRAYERS. The Bible tells us we should pray continually in the Holy Spirit (1 Thessalonians 5:16–18; Jude 20). Not all Christians understand this admonition the same way. At the very least, though, it means we should continually allow the Holy Spirit to lead us in prayer.

Salvation restores communion with God through Christ. So it makes sense that prayer is restored communication with God through Christ by the Holy Spirit. Jesus gave us His life by dying on the cross. The Holy Spirit delivers it to us and remains in us to empower every spiritual work in our lives. Prayer is a spiritual work. The Spirit empowers our faith, He empowers our ability to serve, He empowers our study of God's Word, and He empowers our prayer life. We would not be able to pray in faith without the Holy Spirit.

Without the Spirit our prayers would just be the desperate pleadings of confused and fearful people. Without the Spirit we would have no hope of praying from God's viewpoint. But when we take courage and proclaim the promises of God, not to manipulate God but to worship Him, it is the Holy Spirit that is praying through us. Praying in the Spirit means believing God is good no matter what happens. Prayer that focuses on others, even during hardship, invites the Holy Spirit's leading.

The power in prayer is not in our ability to speak boldly or eloquently; it's in the power of the Spirit who prays though us.

However, the Spirit does not necessarily empower our prayer to be more eloquent, exuberant, or lengthy. These are things we tend to add to our prayers for reasons that don't have anything to do with worshiping and submitting to God. Praying in the Spirit is an act of worshipful submission that any believing child can do. It comes from a heart that adores God and kneels before Him. The Holy Spirit will inhabit such prayer no matter how simple it is. And He yearns to build intimacy between the Father and the one who prays in the Spirit continually. The power in prayer is not in our ability to speak boldly or eloquently; it's in the power of the Spirit who prays though us.

All communication involves approach and response. It comes in the form of questions and answers, point and counterpoint, requests and replies, or greetings and good byes. Praying in the Spirit is the same— it's like breathing. As we learn to listen for the Spirit, He will breathe His Word into us. We will take in the breath of the Spirit and exhale our prayers of worship and trust in God for all that we need. The Spirit is as close as our breath. We need not look for Him or shout for Him. He will inhabit every word and every thought that honors God with humble submission. And He will plead our case to the Father with prayers that we alone cannot pray nor even comprehend (Romans 8:26).

GOD STRENGTHENS US BY WORKING IN US THROUGH FAITH. My definition of faith is this: faith is giving God permission to run your life. At its most basic level, that's what faith is—you just let go of your demands and all bargaining with God. Your prayers are focused on God's will and your readiness to seek it and respond to it.

That kind of faith doesn't come naturally; it's supernatural. The Spirit must build it up in us as He leads us to exercise faith against the devil, the world, and our self-centered nature. By nature we trust ourselves most. But the Spirit reminds us where we come from. We come from the dust and a fallen human race. The Spirit also reminds us that, in Christ, we belong to God and are being transformed to be like Him.

The Spirit calls us into a battle between these two natures. It is a struggle between our flesh and our reborn spirit that requires faith to win daily victories. Just as lifting weights builds physical strength as your muscles work against resistance, so trusting God in the midst of temptation, crisis, or pain builds faith as God shows Himself strong and faithful on your behalf. When you are being challenged, pray the prayer of faith and wait for God's faithfulness. The cry of your soul will be changed to peaceful trust in God.

GOD STRENGTHENS US THROUGH RELATIONSHIPS WITH PEOPLE. If all things serve God for our good (Romans 8:28), then God also uses the people who touch our lives to accomplish His purposes in us. This includes believers who share the same Spirit of life with us and unbelievers who share the same need for a Savior with us. God can use anything and anyone to enlarge His presence in our lives and strengthen our service to Him. We should surround ourselves with Christ-centered people who can lift us up in prayer and encouragement. We should also be in relationship with those who haven't put trust in Christ yet so the Spirit can speak to them through us and strengthen us through our service to them.

The power of the gospel flows through the conduit of relationships.

The power of the gospel flows through the conduit of relationships (1 John 4:9–11). And as it flows it strengthens and deepens those relationships. But we must recognize that there is no true relationship without service. Sacrificial availability builds the trust that deep relationships require. We cannot depend on our stand on biblical truth alone to earn trust with people. Communicating love through our actions, as an outgrowth of our love for Christ, will create this trust and provide a place for the Spirit to work miracles in people's hearts, including ours.

We can use this battle plan God gives us to win victory. But if we don't stay connected to our spiritual supply line, we will become weak and unable to keep up the fight.

> *Finally, my brethren, be strong in the Lord and in the power of His might. Put on the whole armor of God, that you may be able to stand against the wiles of the devil. For we do not wrestle against flesh and blood, but against principalities, against powers, against the rulers of the darkness of this age, against spiritual* hosts *of wickedness in the heavenly places.* Ephesians 6:10–12 (NKJV)

For Review, Teaching, or Discussion

1. What are the three aspects of our battle with our enemies?

2. How does God prepare and lead us to victory in spiritual battles?

3. How does God continually strengthen us to keep up the fight and finish the course?

4. Are you willing to accept the challenge and responsibility of discipling your children?

5. Are you willing to seek help and join with other parents in your community?

part two
the expedition

"WHEN OUR CHILDREN RECOGNIZE GOD AS THE
PRIMARY PURSUIT OF OUR LIVES AND THE SOURCE
OF OUR PEACE AND STRENGTH, THEY WILL BEGIN
TO DESIRE THOSE THINGS FOR THEMSELVES."

chapter five

becoming God-centered parents
how do I raise my children to become like God?

A VIEW OF THE ROAD AHEAD:
- *Experiencing God's fulfillment*
- *Learning the power principles*
- *Check points for reflection*

I often have the opportunity to share with parents the vision of becoming like God. As we talk, I usually find an interesting motivation in their hearts. At first, they'll say something like, "I want my children to be like God. I want them to have His nature—His character." And then they'll say, "Most of all, I want them to be fulfilled."

Do you see the basic truth in that last statement? Becoming like God is more than God's desire for us and our children; it's how we experience true fulfillment, the fulfillment of whom we are meant to be.

> *Becoming like God is how we experience true fulfillment, the fulfillment of whom we are meant to be.*

Our becoming like God is for *us*, not for Him. It's for our benefit and His joy. That is so much like the loving fatherhood of God! Just like you, He is happy when His children are fulfilled.

Children Should Be Fulfilled

It isn't a coincidence that parents will consistently arrive at this conclusion about fulfillment. As parents surrender to God's desire for their children and themselves, their hearts lead them to this truth: we'll never be fulfilled as individuals until we take on the nature of God. That's why we were created. The world is full of distractions, and our busy lives can cloud our awareness of how empty we are without God's presence in us. We may not recognize the real reasons why we feel so unfulfilled, but in Ephesians, Paul reminds us why we were made:

> *We'll never be fulfilled as individuals until we take on the nature of God.*

> *I know that you heard about him, and you are in him, so you were taught the truth that is in Jesus. You were taught to leave your old self— to stop living the evil way you lived before. That old self becomes worse, because people are fooled by the evil things they want to do. But you were taught to be made new in your hearts, to become a new person.* That new person is made to be like God. Ephesians 4:21–24 (NCV; emphasis added)

God has called those who follow Him to become *like* Him—to be filled with Him, fully and completely transformed by Him. Remember that your children are generally going to become like you, just as Jesus turned out exactly like His Father.

So how do you raise your children to become like God? The answer is for *you* to become like God. You've learned that discipling your children begins with your being a disciple. It's very difficult to teach your children one thing while you're living something completely different,

because the best lessons they'll learn
are what you model.

You don't have to be a perfect
model of God; Jesus has already
provided us with that. If you expect
perfection, you could end up
condemning yourself when you

*It's very difficult to teach
your children one thing
while you're living some-
thing completely different.*

fail—which isn't a role you'd want to model. Instead, you should
demonstrate to your children the all-consuming *desire* to be like Jesus.

Remember that a true disciple is one who wants to become like his
or her master. You want your children to know that your first priorities
as a parent are:

1. To become like Christ
2. To help them become like Christ

They need to see how pursuing the character of Christ fulfills and
completes you. As your children see you grow spiritually by actively
pursuing the character of Christ, they'll begin to understand that the real
reason you are growing is because God is actively working in you.

Paul refers to believers in Ephesians 2:10 as "God's workmanship"
(NIV), but we have a part in the process as well: God wants us to cooperate with the Holy Spirit's work in us. The work will eventually get
done whether we cooperate or not. Jesus bought and paid for our rescue
and restoration; God is committed to glorifying and beautifying everyone who belongs to Jesus. But we'll have a lot more joy in our lives, and
we'll be more useful to God's purposes in the world if we'll just partner
with Him instead of resisting Him.

And we have a blueprint for that partnership: the Word of God,
which, in his letter to the Colossians (1:26–28), Paul calls:

> . . . the mystery that has been kept hidden for ages and generations, but
> is now disclosed to the saints. To them God has chosen to make known

among the Gentiles the glorious riches of this mystery, which is Christ in you, the hope of glory. We proclaim him, admonishing and teaching everyone with all wisdom, so that we may present everyone perfect in Christ (NIV).

The Seven Pursuits of Godly Parents

A life of trusting surrender to God's work in our lives involves actively pursuing Him. In the chapters that follow, we'll look closely at seven ways God calls us to pursue Him. One short chapter will be devoted to each pursuit, and each chapter will include an exercise to help make the lesson more meaningful.

To preview, parents who pursue God's character are becoming:

1. people of the Spirit
2. people of worship
3. people of the Word
4. people of prayer
5. people of faith
6. people of hope
7. people of love

As followers of Christ, we should desire these seven characteristics— but this desire can only arise in our hearts as our trust in God's love makes Him increasingly attractive to us. When our children recognize God as the primary pursuit of our lives and the source of our peace and strength, they will begin to desire those things for themselves.

A life of trusting surrender to God's work in our lives involves actively pursuing Him.

Chart your own course with these seven pursuits before you try teaching them to your children. As you improve your understanding of the pursuits, let your desire be for God to invade new areas of your heart and bring you to a deeper level of commitment to Him.

check
point

Let's prepare for the material in the coming chapters by completing the following exercises. Try to quiet your mind, and ask God to give you a listening heart.

Exercise 1

Ask God to show you the pursuits in your past that have been more important to you than your desire to be like Jesus. Make a list below of anything that comes to mind. As you do this, don't let the enemy accuse you; we all need to take inventory of ourselves occasionally. Just have a humble heart, and accept how the Holy Spirit works in you.

Look at what you just wrote, and confess to God your agreement with Him that these things are sin—the same sin Paul says, in Hebrews 12:1, can so easily entangle us. Ask God to reclaim His place as Lord over every area of your life, and believe with confidence that God will joyfully respond as you repent. Then accept God's forgiveness for these sins. Use the space below to chart this course.

Now find and read Matthew 6:33 in your Bible.

Ask God right now to replace your desire for personal comfort with His compassion for people. Ask Him to give you eyes to see what He sees. Ask Him to give you His heart to love others and the faith to do what He tells you to do.

Exercise 2

Feeling disappointment toward God is a common experience for most people. Take a few moments to think about and list the times in your life when you have felt abandoned or let down by God.

Now find and read Hebrews 13:5–6 and Psalm 27.

You've probably read the poem "Footprints in the Sand." This moving poem has become very well known over the last sixty years, and it's even touched the lives of many nonreligious people. It speaks powerfully to us because it offers hope in the midst of troubled times. Most of the time, while God is working in our lives, we are walking with Him; but there can be especially rough times when we are tempted to feel abandoned. During these times, God is actually carrying us.

I urge you to express, often and out loud, your confidence in God, and thank Him for the assurance that He will never leave you nor forsake you. Do this now in the space below.

Now find and read Matthew 16:24–27.

In the space below, write a note to God, telling Him how much you desire to become like Him. As you write, express your willingness to surrender your life to Him.

As your commitment to pursue God grows, remember that discipleship is a journey with Jesus, who was the most patient of teachers. Paul called his own journey a race that had been set before him (1 Corinthians 9:24; 2 Timothy 4:7). This race is a marathon, not a hundred-yard dash. It's a lifelong adventure, and just like any race, there will be many places where you can quit but only one place where you can finish.

Be patient and trust God to disciple you as He chooses. Use the life He gives you to learn how to journey well so you can finish well.

chapter six

God-centered parents are people of the Spirit

what does it mean to be born of the Spirit?

A VIEW OF THE ROAD AHEAD:

- *Being born of the Spirit*
- *Dying to our sin nature*

You can't begin the pursuit of God's nature and character without being born into His family. Look at the third chapter of John, and you'll find that Jesus helped Nicodemus understand exactly what this means.

Nicodemus was confused when Jesus told him that in order to see the kingdom of heaven he must be born again. Nicodemus couldn't conceive that Jesus meant a *different kind* of birth than being delivered from a mother's womb.

Born of the Spirit

How can I be born of the Spirit? Nicodemus wondered. But Jesus reminded him that there is flesh, and then there is spirit (John 3:6). Just as we are born of flesh into our temporary earthly families, we must have a spiritual birth to enter God's eternal heavenly family. This spiritual birth takes place instantly when we put our faith in Christ for the forgiveness of our sins and trust Him with our lives and our future.

> When we cry out to God He adopts us as His children and puts His Spirit in us.

In chapter four of his letter to the Ephesians, Paul explains something about the new birth that isn't so obvious to many Christians: this spiritual new birth in Christ is actually an adoption. Paul says that when we cry out to God He adopts us as His children and puts His Spirit in us. Then we can call Him, "Abba Father," which affectionately means "Dad."

But that's just the beginning! Just as adopted children should expect to share equally in their heritage with the natural children of their adoptive parents, God's adopted children become heirs with Christ to everything God possesses. Everything! Jesus is the only natural (begotten) Son of God (see John 1:18, 3:16; 1 John 4:9). We who are made spiritually alive by trusting in what Jesus did for us on the cross are now adopted children of God (Romans 8:17; Galatians 4:7).

Our rebirth in the Spirit isn't a natural birth; it's actually a spiritual adoption (see Romans 8:23; Ephesians 1:5–6).

A lot of people think every person is born a child of God, but the Bible makes it clear that isn't true. So if being born of the flesh doesn't make you a child of God, what does it make you? It makes you a creation of God. There's a big difference between the two.

In 2 Corinthians 1:21–22, Paul says if you are an adopted child of God, He has placed His seal of sonship upon you. Paul's first readers would have understood a *seal* to be a mark of ownership. Back then, when a king or landlord owned something, he could cut or burn his family crest onto the item or property. Documents were marked with a crest by pressing them into hot wax. Likewise, God has claimed everyone who is in Christ as His. But what does God use for a seal? Paul explains that God has put His Spirit in you as His seal of rightful ownership.

When God looks at someone who has His Spirit in them, He says,

"That one is mine!" We must be born again of His Spirit (John 3:5) to become God's children and then begin our journey of becoming like Him.

John 3:6 says, "That which is born of the flesh is flesh" (NASB). This means we are born of water when we are delivered from our mothers' womb; but because of sin, our spirits are dead to God (Ephesians 2:1). By confessing Christ as our Savior, His death and resurrection restore us to life. In Christ, we are no longer children of death—we are children of God.

Verse 6 continues by saying, "That which is of the Spirit is spirit." This means without adoption into God's family, we remain orphaned by our sinful nature, living a life that is of this world. With our adoption comes a new life—a new life born of God's Spirit (2 Corinthians 5:16–21).

Filled with the Spirit

We are born into this new life—a life in the Spirit—but very few Christians really understand what this means.

First, let's get the facts straight. The moment we put our trust in Christ for our salvation (as opposed to trusting in our own good works) we cross from death to life. It's not a long, drawn-out process; it happens instantly. We are suddenly made alive in the Spirit. However, there is a gradual change in how our lives begin to reflect what is already true about the new us.

Notes from Benny's Journal
"TRUE OWNERSHIP"

When I talk to teenagers about new life in the Spirit, I start by asking, "If some-one had deposited a million dollars into a bank in your name on the day you were born, what would that make you?" After they think for a few seconds, they usually respond, "A millionaire!"

After I agree with their answer, I pose another question: "On the day you were born, how much did you understand about what it means to be a millionaire?" They usually say they understood nothing. I then explain that this is the way it is with us as newborn Christians. When we are reborn in Christ, we receive ownership of treasures beyond our understanding. We each receive the gift of salvation, the presence of the Holy Spirit, a divine destiny, and an unimaginable inheritance. It takes time for us to begin to understand who we are when we're reborn in Christ and what we are to become.

Ephesians 5:18 tells us not to be drunk with wine, as that is excess; but instead be filled with the Holy Spirit. In other words, don't allow yourself to be lead by the influences of wine or anything else that your flesh might crave. Instead, be controlled by God's Spirit. Paul says we are alive *in* the Spirit; now live *by* the Spirit.

> *When we are reborn in Christ, we receive ownership of treasures beyond our understanding*

If you read Ephesians 5:18 in the Greek translation, it says you are commanded to trust in and be so dependent upon the Spirit that you are continually filled up inside with the Spirit. If you only trust yourself to meet the demands and confrontations of life, you will inevitably become filled with a spirit of discontentment, deception, and depression. You will then become angry. Anger and continual confrontation with everything that gets in your way will control you and define who you are. That kind of life is what separates us from God.

You can set your heart free from the anger that results from contending with all the evil in this world by trusting God daily, even in your disappointments. This will make your heart submissive to the Holy Spirit. The fruit of the Spirit will be produced in you and pour out of you (Galatians 5:22–25).

Empowered by the Spirit

Ephesians 3:19 says:

May you experience the love of Christ, though it is so great you will never fully understand it. Then you will be filled with the fullness of life and power that comes from God. (NLT; emphasis added)

And 2 Peter 1:3 says:

As we know Jesus better, his divine power gives us everything we need *for living a godly life.* (NLT; emphasis added)

Now read 2 Timothy 1:7. It says:

For God has not given us a spirit of fear and timidity, but of power, *love, and self-discipline.* (NLT; emphasis added)

The more you learn to submit moment by moment to the Holy Spirit's leading, the more powerful will be your life *by* the Spirit.

Second Corinthians 5:17 says that old things will pass away and new things will come. As part of God's family, everything in our lives is made new. In Christ we are living spirits who can know God in the person of our Savior. We are made spiritually alive to God in a way that continually draws us to Him.

Anger and continual confrontation with everything that gets in your way will control you and define who you are.

In this world, we'll find ourselves fighting a daily battle for the souls of our children and for our own souls as well. The toughest battle we'll face as Christians is the battle between the physical desires of our flesh and our life of submission to the Spirit. Paul speaks passionately to us about this internal spiritual battle in Romans 5–8. He teaches with such honesty by exposing his own struggle. The very man through whom God chose to give us so much of His inspired Word confessed:

For what I will to do, that I do not practice; but what I hate, that I do....O wretched man that I am! Who will deliver me from this body of death? Romans 7:15, 24 (NKJV)

Paul was set free to live according to the Spirit because of what Christ did. If Paul had lived according to the flesh, the constant battle between flesh and spirit would have held him in bondage to guilt, fear, and anger. Instead, he rejoices that his trust in Christ sets him free in the midst of the battle (Romans 8:1–2).

When we are born of the Spirit, a battle begins within us. Jesus assures us this battle has already been won, and we can experience this victory if we face the battle the way He did. Oh, yes, Jesus battled as well! But Jesus overcame by His submission and obedience to the Father who is Spirit (John 4:24).

> *The toughest battle we'll face as Christians is the battle between the physical desires of our flesh and our life of submission to the Spirit.*

Some might say, "Yeah, but Jesus was the holy Son of God! He knew God in a way we can't." That's true, but Hebrews 4:15 says that in His humanity, Jesus was tempted in every way we are tempted. How could that be true if Jesus, the Son of God, possessed resources that we don't have in order to overcome those temptations? Remember, as Paul says in Philippians 2:7, Jesus, the Son of God, chose to take upon Himself the limitations of all men so He could be the redeemer for all men (Galatians 4:4–5). In other words, He limited Himself to life in the world as we live it in order to be as we are—except that He was *without sin.* He came into the world physically the same way we all do—by human birth. He lived daily, trusting in the faithfulness of His heavenly Father the same way we are free to do if we believe. So Jesus was not only the perfect picture of God, He was also what God wants us to be. The Father showed us who He truly was by sending His Son to live and die for the glory of God.

Notes from Benny's Journal
"KILLING OUR SIN NATURE"

*I like to share another story with teenagers about gaining **power** over our old sin nature. I call it "How to Kill Your Old Man." They initially think I'm talking about their dads! You might laugh, but I can tell you that killing the **old man** at home has crossed some of their minds!*

*I then explain that I'm talking about the old man each of us **used** to be before we gave our lives to Christ. That's the old man I want to and must kill in order to live in submission and obedience to the Father, just like Jesus did. Jesus said we would have to kill our old man every day. He said we must deny ourselves, take up our cross daily, and follow Him (Luke 9:23).*

A preacher who is older and wiser than me once said, "I know I believe in the resurrection because the old man in me I killed yesterday got back up again today! Every day I kill him, and he gets right back up again!" I understood what he was saying. We all have an old man; he keeps hanging around inside of us, competing for control in our lives. Killing the old man daily is a way of life. It is a cross we must carry every day.

Killing the Old Man

We also have the new man in us who was born of the Holy Spirit. He is now present in us as God's gift and the seal of our salvation. You must begin each day with a conscious effort to acknowledge the old man in you, and then deny him any authority in your life. We do that by first remembering who we are—by claiming the truth about our new identity in Christ. Then we submit to the Holy Spirit continually so He guides us continually. As you grow spiritually, you will learn to hear His voice in every situation and have faith to obey Him.

Finally, the Holy Spirit makes God's Word come alive in us (see John 14:26), and we learn to trust the Spirit so much that He empowers us to do as Paul instructs:

You were taught to leave your old self—to stop living the evil way you lived before. That old self becomes worse, because people are fooled by the evil things they want to do. But you were taught to be made new in your hearts, to become a new person. That new person is made to be like God—made to be truly good and holy. Ephesians 4:22–24 (NCV)

God-centered parents pursue the Spirit in order to be led by Him. If you live this way consistently, God will inspire your children to follow you as you follow the Spirit. Soon, they will begin to respond to the Spirit's leading directly.

check point

1. Take a few minutes to reflect upon your second birth experience. Write down your memory of when you committed your life to Jesus.

2. Ask a Christian friend to share his or her born-again experience. What are some of the similarities and differences to your own experience?

3. Describe how your life is different since you chose to follow Jesus.

4. Describe how the Holy Spirit in you has guided your life.

5. What has the Holy Spirit revealed to you about your relationship to Jesus?

6. Give examples of how the Holy Spirit has convicted you of sin in your life and how He has convinced you to do the right thing.

7. In your own words, ask the Holy Spirit to live in you, reveal Himself to you, and guide your life.

chapter seven

God-centered parents are people of worship

how do I live what I believe?

A VIEW OF THE ROAD AHEAD:

- *Defining worship*
- *Pursuing God*

The more something is worth to us, the more we want it and the more we worship it. Worship, then, is declaring the worth of something and pursuing it. But what do we call something we value more than God? God calls it idolatry.

Notes from Benny's Journal
"RUBBERNECKING"

*Growing up in the South, I heard of a certain type of person called a **rubberneck**. Sometimes, I'd hear, "Hey man! You're rubbernecking!" It sounds like one of Jeff Foxworthy's redneck terms, doesn't it?*

But it's a great description for someone who always turns his head as he passes by something he wants. My teenaged head turned many times to follow a passing Corvette! That kind of behavior happens naturally because the things we value the most are what most quickly catch and hold our attention.

The Spirit of Idolatry

It's easy to criticize the ancients who worshiped household gods that were represented by figurines, or to point the finger at the Israelites, who

Worship is declaring the worth of something and pursuing it.

made a golden calf just after their miraculous deliverance by God as they walked across the Red Sea on dry ground in their escape from Egypt. We hear about these ancient times in church and think, *Could these people be any more ridiculous? How could they do such things after God was so powerfully present with them?*

Maybe we walk out of church and gaze at some of the cars that other people are getting into. Maybe we go home to whatever meal we can assemble out of the fridge, and we feel slighted because we can't afford to eat out this week. We want a bigger house, more money to live a richer lifestyle, and more time off from work to travel instead of just taking the family to our parents' house for Christmas every year.

To want something—even a high-priced material thing—isn't wrong in itself. The spirit of idolatry sets in when we are so distracted by discontent with what we have that we lose our passion for God. Anything that replaces even a small part of the worship, devotion, or attention that should belong to God has become an idol, and God hates it. He loves us and wants us too much to let an idol come between us and Him. The truth is, we are no less prone to idolatry than the ancient people.

The True God of Idolatry

In Jeremiah 7, God rebukes Israel for turning from Him and worshiping Baal. Many people in Israel were even sacrificing their children to this pagan god. Again, we tend to think no one today would do such a thing or worship pagan gods, but if you do a little research into why ancient people worshiped Baal, Molech, and similar gods, you'll soon realize that most of our modern society worships in the same way. We just don't usually give a personal name to our gods.

Anything that replaces even a small part of the worship, devotion, or attention that should belong to God has become an idol, and God hates it.

The ancients sacrificed to pagan gods and worshiped them in temples in order to gain favor and prosperity. Baal was even called the god of prosperity and pleasure. One of the ways the gods were worshiped was for followers to have sex with prostitutes in the temples of these gods. So you see, it wasn't really the gods that were being worshiped; what the unfaithful people of Israel (and other ancient people) were really valuing more than God were personal well-being, prosperity, and pleasure. Their devotion to God wasn't as great as their commitment to their own comfort. They turned away from God in order to get these things because, like so many of us today, they were discontent with God's authority over them.

The ancient people probably didn't turn to the pagan lifestyle overnight. Their divided hearts gradually weakened their hold on the things of God until everything in their lives represented paganism. The ancients may have superstitiously believed they would be blessed by sacrificing their children to a pagan god, but in today's reality, our society is no different from the ancient world. Devotion to God and His purposes have taken a backseat to the pursuit of personal peace and affluence in American society. Even in Christian homes, there are many children learning to value popularity and prosperity more than God's will for their lives.

In essence, we are sacrificing our children to western materialism by putting our prosperity before their spiritual needs. We may be teaching them about God, but we are not seeking His kingdom first. We're

We are sacrificing our children to Western materialism by putting our prosperity before their spiritual needs.

communicating a compromised message to them. Our message of idolatry comes from our own hearts.

Ask yourself this question: *if I were given the power to give my child a life as either a millionaire movie star or a missionary who depends on God every day for survival, which life would I choose to give her?* The comfort and self-fulfillment many children in America are being taught to prefer can actually be the seeds of death—physically and spiritually (Proverbs 14:12).

Whatever name men give to the things they desire enough to worship, their real god is still themselves. Self-worshiping men have always turned from God to the god of this world in order to get what *they* want. Self-interest is the religion of the world, and its god is anything that brings immediate satisfaction. This blind ambition keeps us and our children from God (2 Corinthians 4:4).

Worship, by the way, is part of everyone's life. We all have our eyes and ears fixed on something that shapes who we are. What our lives reflect shows what we truly worship.

We all live in the world, so we are all vulnerable to the influence of its religion. This influence, plus the weakness of the flesh and struggle

Self-interest is the religion of the world, and its god is anything that brings immediate satisfaction.

with sin, makes it very common to find pockets of pagan lifestyle in the lives of Christians. We don't worship Baal, per se, but we are religiously pursuing the same prosperity and pleasure that Baal worshipers did. Francis Schaeffer called it a religion of personal peace and affluence. As long as this is what motivates us—not the glory of God and His purposes—it doesn't matter how often we go to church, how many church committees we serve, how many Christian books we write, or how loud we sing in worship. As long as there is anything we want more than obeying the voice of God in our lives, then we aren't living as the people of God.

This doesn't mean God will turn His back on us. God is faithful even when we aren't. But God will discipline His children as any loving parent would. God's discipline is always right and usually tough.

We Live What We Believe

Many professing Christians may not even know they are practicing atheism. They go to church on Sunday, and sometimes talk about Jesus, but they don't desire time alone with God. They don't have any hunger to read His Word or share it with others. They don't trust God enough to be honest with close Christian friends about the sin and heartache in their lives. They don't seek to be led by the Spirit so they can respond when He opens their eyes to a need. Most of the time they live like God doesn't exist at all; or perhaps they just don't have time for Him.

I'm not pointing my finger at anyone in particular. I've been in ministry all my adult life, and my own heart has become cold and distant at times. But we all need to guard our hearts, especially when our lives are terribly hectic or burdened with trouble and disappointment. How we decide to deal with life when it *isn't* easy to follow Christ can more quickly form habits than when times are good and gentle. Habits, whether good or bad, collectively form a lifestyle.

The lifestyle of God's people should be one of continual prayer, taking every thought captive for Christ (2 Corinthians 10:5). True Christian people of worship will put away idolatry, and they will desire to be like God more than anything else. They are known by their desire for God. They look to Him and listen for His voice. The number one

The number one desire of their lives is to be near Him so much that they become like Him. That's what it means to worship God above all other things.

desire of their lives is to be near Him so much that they become like Him. That's what it means to worship God above all other things.

A Reason to Worship

The reason God calls us to worship Him is so we can see Him clearly. If you want to be like someone, you need to spend time with him and really get to know him. In worship, God reveals Himself in a special way. We do get to see God revealed in Christ, but when we worship we get to experience God's presence and see Him through our spiritual eyes. That's why the Scriptures tell us that God is a Spirit, and that we must worship Him in spirit and in truth (John 4:24). When we seek God in spirit and truth we are recalling His greatness while praising His goodness and the sharing of His Word. His nature and character are seen, valued, and desired. God truly inhabits the praises of His people.

Whether we and our children reflect this image of God or the values of the world depends on how well we keep our eyes and our ears focused on God.

One way worship works is like a giant camera taking a picture of God. Imagine yourself looking through a camera that is out of focus. Many times in my life, the pressures of my world and the lust of my flesh have distorted my view of God—He was completely out of focus in my life. My relationship to Him and the life He called me to were a big blur.

In worship, while seeking God's presence and celebrating His love, His true nature and His character are refocused in our lives. We get a more perfect picture of what He is like and what we are to be like; we reflect what we hear, see, or understand. Whether we and our children reflect this image of God or the values of the world depends on how well we keep our eyes and our ears focused on God.

Notes from Benny's Journal
"REFLECTION OF SOUND"

My wife, Marilou, and I had the joy of sharing Christ with a sixteen-year-old deaf student named Heather. Years later in 1995, in spite of being deaf, Heather Whitestone (now Heather McCullough) became Miss America.

I once asked Heather a question, and I'll never forget her response because it illustrates so well how Christians become a reflection of what we understand about God. I asked her how much she could actually hear. Heather replied, "You can tell how much a deaf person can hear by listening to her talk."

I thought for a long time about what she said and tried to make sense of her answer. Then it struck me what she was saying: since a deaf person's hearing is distorted, her words are distorted as well. The sound she is making with her voice is a reflection of what she is hearing.

This dynamic holds true spiritually as well. If we are a poor reflection of God to our children, they are being led to become a poor reflection of who He is.

God reveals Himself to us in response to our uncompromised worship of Him. When Moses came down from the mountain, his face glowed with the glory that shined upon him from God's presence. That is a picture of what happens when we worship God in Spirit and in truth. God will respond by giving us a true picture of who He is and what we are to become.

Many times in my life I have prayed, "God, when my children are with me, I want them to see that I've been with You." The more our children see us living out this kind of worship for God every day, the more that light will shine in their lives.

check
point

In a previous exercise, we tested our leadership style by thinking about how we would react to certain conflicts of will with our children.

This is important because the Bible warns us not to exasperate our children to the point that we no longer have their attention (see Ephesians 6:4; Colossians 3:21). We can force them to listen while we talk to them, but that doesn't mean they are willingly hearing us.

We can increase the likelihood that we'll be the primary influence on our children by making them feel that their hearts and lives are safe with us.

While we have their attention, it is also important to make sure that what they see and hear in us is a humble and consistent commitment to follow Christ.

Now let's examine how tightly we are holding on to the *things* in our lives as opposed to how tightly we are holding on to Jesus. Are there any idols in your life? Using this two-part exercise, let's find out.

Part One

Imagine that you are traveling alone or on personal business, and your small charter plane has crash-landed in the remote mountains of a foreign country. The pilot is dead, the radio is smashed, your leg is broken, there are no provisions, and there's no way to keep warm as night approaches. You know you're going to freeze to death before anyone realizes you're missing. After a couple of hours of panic and shock, you begin to make peace with the likely result of your situation, and you begin to think about your family. As tears fill your eyes, you wish you could tell each of them something. You ask God to let them know you love them, and that you wanted so much for them. God whispers back to your heart, "You can say whatever you want to them— write it down, and it will be treasured by your family for generations." You look up at the sky and breathe deeply, realizing that night will fall in about two hours and the temperature will drop about fifty degrees. You painfully manage to get a tablet of paper and a pen, and you begin to write.

Go to a quiet place—away from people—and write your last words to your family. Write a letter to each person. The length of the letter doesn't matter; unpacking your heart to them is what's important. It's also important that you think of these letters as the last words your family will ever receive from you.

Remember that you're dying, so you may as well be honest and vulnerable, as long as what you say benefits *them*. If you're reading this book hoping to gain something that will make you a better parent, then you need to do this exercise before you continue reading.

Now, put the book down and go write.

Part Two

The first part of this exercise was intended to focus your mind and heart on what is most important in your life; our dying words have a way of defining that for us. If you're a follower of Christ, you no doubt wrote words that will encourage your family's devotion to Christ.

But I want you to get quiet again, think hard about your family life, and try to answer these questions:

1. How often has your family seen your true heart? How often have the things you've done with your family and the words you've spoken to them come from the same heart of surrender to God's will that wrote your dying words?

2. Suppose I told you to give the letters you just wrote to your family and let them read them. Do you feel any hesitation or anxiety at the thought of them actually reading what you wrote? If so, why?

3. Is there anything in your life that, if compared with your letters, would make you feel like a hypocrite or a phony? For instance, have you

spent most of your time chasing financial success or selfish pursuits because you feel insecure or because you covet things you don't really need in order to serve Christ? You probably wouldn't feel free to let your family read your letters unless they actually were your last words. Any hesitation you feel to give your dying words to your family may indicate that there is some level of idolatry in your life. You may be holding back because your conscience is telling you to be honest and live what you say you believe.

Ask God to show you what you are holding on to that doesn't match up with a heart that dies to self and surrenders to Him. Write about what He shows you and then confess it.

4. Ask God to loosen your grip on idolatrous things and tighten your grip on Him. Freedom from idolatry may not come easily or imme- diately, but keep an attitude of repentance and keep praying. God will wrestle with your heart and make you strong for Him. Ask Him to reveal Himself to your spirit as you worship Him in Spirit and truth so you can become like Him.

chapter eight

God-centered parents are people of the Word

am I honoring Christ with my life and the words I speak?

A VIEW OF THE ROAD AHEAD:

- *Defining words of life*
- *Searching for truth*
- *Avoiding mere opinions*

One day near the end of His ministry, Jesus was teaching in Capernaum. He told His followers He would not be performing any more miracles; He would no longer be feeding or healing them. Most of the crowd became confused and offended by what Jesus preached, so they decided to go home and they didn't follow Jesus anymore. Here is what happened next:

> *Then Jesus said to the twelve, "Do you also want to go away?" But Simon Peter answered Him, "Lord, to whom shall we go? You have the words of eternal life." John 6:67–68* (NKJV)

Peter said something about Jesus that day that I want people to say about me: "He speaks life and truth."

To be "people of the Word" means we're not people of *opinion*. We all have opinions, but that doesn't mean we should speak them or have the right to share them. Second Corinthians 10:5 says we are to take every thought captive to Christ. We should ask ourselves, *When I share my opinions, am I honoring Christ or myself? Am I saying what Christ would say?*

Words of Truth and Life

In reality, how much life can our opinions give to others? What good does it do anyone to respect our opinions if they don't come from the words of life? If we are people of the Spirit and people of worship, it follows that we should be people who speak God's words. The words we speak into the lives of others should be more than just our opinions.

Where do we get words of life and truth that others can be confident are more than just opinions? The obvious answer is from God Himself, because God doesn't just *know* all truth; He *establishes* all truth. God doesn't have opinions—He proclaims His will. So a person who has the words of life and truth is a person who speaks the words of God.

> *Our children should see that we walk with God in our relationship with Jesus and that we hunger for His words of life.*

The Scripture tells us to study God's Word diligently, to hide it in our hearts and meditate on it day and night. We should never let it depart from our mouths, and we should do all it says. Depending on the truth of God's Word lights our path, keeps us from sin, and strengthens us to proclaim the truth about God's redeeming lost humanity though Christ. Jesus came in order to bring us into a relationship, not a religion. Our children should see that we walk with God in our relationship with Jesus and that we hunger for His words of life. They need to see that we aren't fooled by the philosophies of this world (Colossians 2:8).

The Search for Truth

The search for the ultimate truth is a great mystery that has burdened every man since the beginning of time. Throughout history, man has looked for one complete answer. This mystery involves three questions:

1. What is the greatest power?
2. What is the deepest knowledge?
3. What is the meaning of life?

Seeking answers to these questions is the reason all religions have developed. That's what most religion is—it's the human pursuit of connection with the highest power, the deepest knowledge, and the most abundant life. Man instinctively knows he doesn't have any answers to the mystery on his own, so he searches until he finds something that seems to provide answers. Satan helps man along with just enough discoveries to keep him in bondage to the struggle for more power, more knowledge, and more abundant life.

Jesus is the answer to this mystery and all of man's pursuits. He said:

"I am the way, the truth, and the life. No one comes to the Father except through Me. If you had known Me, you would have known My Father also; and from now on you know Him and have seen Him." John 14:6–7 (NKJV)

Jesus didn't come just to tell us the answers to the great mystery; He *is* the fulfillment of the mystery. When Jesus says He is "the way, the truth, and the life," He is proclaiming Himself as the source of the highest power, the deepest knowledge, and the most abundant life. These also correspond to His threefold office as King, Prophet, and Priest.

God wants us to seek power, knowledge, and life in Him, not create them for ourselves. Chasing the mystery our way only results in a vast variety of opinions and jealously guarded religions.

By nature we are like the Israelites, who built a golden calf to worship because they preferred opinions they were familiar with over the new revelation Moses was receiving on the mountain of God. Later, Moses put three things in the ark of the covenant to show that the God of Abraham was the one true source of all power, knowledge, and life: Aaron's rod, the tablets of the law, and the pot of manna.

If we want more than opinions to give to our children, we must receive greater revelation from God. God has sent us Jesus to give us (and our children) what we need. Jesus sent us the Spirit in His place to give us power (John 14:16, 16:7). He gave us the knowledge of truth because He is the Word made flesh (John 1:1, 14–15, 8:32, 17:17). And He gave us His life in exchange for our lives, so that we can have the greatest life (1 John 4:9; John 10:10).

Notes from Benny's Journal
"PAYING IT FORWARD"

When my children were young, I would say, "Let me tell you what the Bible says . . .". Sometimes they rolled their eyes as if to say, "Here he goes again!" Maybe your kids do that too; but you have to let that pass because the payoff comes later. God promises that His Word will not return void of any result. I discovered how faithful God is to this promise. My children are grown now, and so many times they have thanked me for going to the Word so much when they were young. It annoyed them back then, because what they wanted was an opinion they could agree or disagree with. They knew being confronted with the authority of God's Word meant accepting or rejecting God because Jesus is the Word.

The Recklessness of Opinions

If our answers don't come from the Word of God, we can't claim they are more than just opinion; they have no more proven value in them than the clothes we're wearing. We think they look good when we're presenting them, but in time, holes will begin to show. Just as our clothes are ours alone, our opinions may not be anyone else's opinions either.

Our opinions can have power though. Opinions can hurt people. So many of us are reckless with the words we speak. Arrogance can make us compulsive, thinking we have the right to speak anything that comes into our minds. But when we speak into someone's life with this attitude, we could end up planting lies, false hope,

We must pursue only the wisdom, power, and life in God's Word as the source of truth we speak into the world.

fear, self-hatred, or any number of deadly things into their souls. We can only be sure of speaking life into others if we are people of the Word of God, who diligently bring every thought captive to Christ and His truth.

We must pursue only the wisdom, power, and life in God's Word as the source of truth we speak into the world.

Notes from Benny's Journal
"LEAD ME TO THE TRUTH"

I never understood what it meant to pursue the Word of God until I understood what God wants: He wants me to think like Him and talk like Him. That's why He gave us the Bible as His Word.

There are too many of us who express deep desire for Jesus in worship, but we never respond to Him by diligently and regularly studying His Word. We go to church and attend conferences, and we listen to Christian radio and teaching tapes, but we don't take time to dig into God's Word by ourselves while praying for the Holy Spirit to lead us into all truth. That is an open door for Satan to lead us into deception.

The apostle John tells us to test every spirit to see if it comes from God (see 1 John 4:1). Satan is a deceiver and a counterfeiter. He comes as an angel of light. But we need the unchanging Word of God as the checkpoint for truth to keep Satan's lies from pulling us off course. It takes no effort to be told the truth, but it does to make truth a part of you. Paul tells us to study God's Word and rightly understand it:

> Be diligent to present yourself approved to God, a worker who doesn't need to be ashamed, correctly teaching the word of truth. 2 Timothy 2:15 (HCSB)

Standing on the Word

I've been asked how I am able to quote Scripture and make reference to it by verse while in conversation and in response to situations. Some people say they could never do that. I used to feel like that when I heard people quoting God's Word. Once God convicted me that I should know His Word, I began to study, memorize, and meditate on it every day. I decided to trust the Bible's promise that the Holy Spirit would bring His Word to my remembrance when I needed it (John 14:26). I realized it would be hard for the Holy Spirit to bring to my remembrance something that wasn't in my memory. Jesus was taught the Scripture as a child by His parents, and He used it powerfully throughout His life.

I once told a group of men I was teaching that, through my spiritual eyes, all I saw in front of me was a big group of babies, sitting in high chairs and crying, "Feed me! Feed me!" We aren't supposed to be mere consumers of teaching ministry; the Bible calls us a priesthood of believers (1 Peter 2:9).

The biblical view of a believer is not someone who just hears and agrees with a truth—he is someone who pursues and stands immovably upon a truth. And as part of a priesthood, we don't just stand, we proclaim the truth we stand on. That level of commitment and responsibility requires us to be more than just familiar with the truth; we must make it a part of us. The point here is that we become people *of* the Word, not just advocates *for* the Word. As a royal priesthood, we are personally responsible for studying and sharing the truth in God's Word.

check
point

If you don't have a regular daily time when you open a Bible and ask the Holy Spirit to lead you into His truth, your assignment is to establish that time each day.

If you're going to follow Jesus and lead your children to follow Him, this is *not* an option. Worshiping Jesus but neglecting His Word is a contradiction. It makes your worship sound false in the Lord's ears.

Start by making a list of all the things you have to do in your daily routine—like eating, bathing, taking out the garbage, watching the news, or anything else you do every day.

Now make another list, only this time put these words at the top of the list: *Study the Bible and meditate on it.*

Start with fifteen minutes, spending time every day alone with God and His Word. This doesn't mean that time in the Word has to come first in the day, but it will begin to nag at you if you let the whole day go by without putting a check next to your number one routine. If you manage to spend time in the Word as a daily routine for thirty days, it will become a habit. And, as I said before, if you nurture a habit long enough, it becomes a lifestyle. Developing the lifestyle is up to you. The power, wisdom, and meaning you will get as a person of the Word is God's promise.

There are many free Bible study plans available to you. Ask your pastor or a friend for help in getting started. If nothing else, a good place to begin is at the beginning of the Bible. Read a couple of chapters in both the Old and New Testaments every day. I like to listen to the Bible on audio CDs when I'm driving.

As you make your Bible reading a habit, you'll find yourself increasing the number of chapters you read; but try keeping the number of chapters the same for both testaments. By the time you finish the Old Testament, you will have read the New Testament three times. Feel free to change your plan, but make your routine a daily one.

Finally, if you really want to disciple yourself well, then make yourself accountable to a friend who will follow the same routine. The object of this assignment is to establish the Word as part of the air you breathe every day. When it becomes that kind of a routine for you, then it really is at the top of your list. In a short time, you'll know yourself as a person of the Word, and you'll be prepared to speak life into the lives of your children and others.

chapter nine

God-centered parents are people of prayer

how can I hear directly from God?

A VIEW OF THE ROAD AHEAD

- *Communicating with God*
- *Seeing the kingdom*

It's difficult to be proud when we're on our knees before God, seeking His help. There's a big difference between kneeling with your guard down and standing with your arms folded and your upper lip stiffened. When we aren't living like people of prayer, the Word, and the Spirit, we naturally slide into a different posture known as self-reliance.

Self-reliance isn't the same thing as spiritual maturity. In fact, self-reliance and an attitude of prayer are opposites.

A mature person . . .	*A self-reliant person . . .*
humbly does what he knows he ought to do;	trusts only himself to do what he chooses to do;
prays because he knows he needs God's power and grace.	says, "I don't need God. I can handle this on my own."

The Adventure of Prayer

I believe the greatest adventures in life come from hearing the voice of God; so clearly, self-reliant people are denying themselves this great adventure. Jesus said in the Gospel of John that His sheep hear His voice, they know His voice, and they follow Him (John 10:27). Prayer is communication with God; it is deliberate, daily, and dynamic. You get quiet and speak to God from your heart, and He begins to speak back to your heart.

But prayer is more than a few moments on your knees or in your car on the way to work. The Bible says to pray continually and without ceasing; maintain a constant attitude of prayer. That doesn't mean talking constantly. A healthy prayer life is about 5 percent talking to God and 95 percent listening for God. The great adventure comes when you hear from God, and you do what He says. It's an adventure because at times it will be exciting, while other times it's unpredictable and even frightening.

Anything God tells His people to do always involves prayer. Without prayer, you wouldn't be able to move forward, but when you obey and you see what God does through you, you will have the most exciting time of your life. After a while, you'll love the adventure so much, you'll need to discipline yourself not to presume too quickly that you are hearing God. The excitement can actually make you behave with haste, which can also open the door to Satan's deceptive ways.

It's important to let God have His own timing for all things. Your response as a person of prayer is to wait, listen, and then respond faithfully and expectantly when God speaks to you.

Notes from Benny's Journal
"A MOST UNLIKELY RESPONSE"

One of my favorite stories about prayer is told by author Beth Moore. She said she was sitting in an airport, reading a book and waiting to board. Her desire is always to pray continually, and at that moment, she prayed, "God I want to hear Your voice. I want to be obedient and do what You say." Just then, an airline employee brought a little old man in a wheelchair to the waiting area. He seemed pretty helpless, and he had very unkempt, long gray hair.

Beth heard the Lord tell her, "Beth, I want you to go over there and comb that man's hair." It was such an oddball idea, Beth felt it couldn't really be God speaking. She tried to continue reading, but then she looked up at the man and immediately felt it again— "Beth, go over there and comb that man's hair. That's what I want you to do."

Thinking "Ooookay," she walked over to the little old man in the wheelchair, and said, "Sir, I'm a Christian, and the Lord's been speaking to me. This may sound weird or a little crazy, but the Lord told me to brush your hair. Will you let me brush your hair?"

The old man's eyes filled with tears. He said, "Thank you so much. My wife is at home; she's an invalid and couldn't travel with me to where I just had surgery. I got out of the hospital this morning. I'm finally going home to my wife, and I've felt so bad all day about the way I look. I would love for you to comb my hair." So Beth got her own hairbrush out, and she fixed the man's hair.

During Beth's flight, one of the attendants came to her and said, "I saw what you did. Can you explain that to me?" Beth said, "I'm a Christian, and it sounds crazy, but I was sitting there and felt like the Lord told me to go and brush that old man's hair."

Beth's adventure with God that day included showing love to a suffering man, which opened the door to telling a flight attendant about Christ. You see, when God calls you to do something—even if it's something you fear—faith will move you past your fear, and God will accomplish what you could have never done on your own.[1]

Author John Eldredge says God is like a wild man: He climbs the most treacherous slopes. Following Him can be scary, but it's incredibly exhilarating to know you have actually heard from God and watched Him work a miracle out of your response to Him. When that occurs, you no longer care how foolish you look or how scared you are.

> *Faith will move you past your fear, and God will accomplish what you could have never done on your own.*

[1] Beth Moore, *Further Still*, Broadman & Holman Publishers, 2004.

It Might Sound Crazy, But . . .

Mark, who works with us in our ministry, tells a story about an experience he had while he and several college students were witnessing on the sidewalks in Birmingham, Alabama. At the end of the day, they were walking back to the van, and Mark was about fifteen feet behind the group. Just as Mark was passing a bar, a huge man of about six eight walked out the bar door. He had long hair and was wearing a Hell's Angels jacket. The guy was big and mean looking, and he had been drinking. He walked out in front of Mark and leaned against a telephone poll. Mark stepped around the man, but then felt the Lord telling him to tell that man God loves him.

Mark immediately thought, *God, that's crazy. I can't say anything to that guy. He'll kill me.* Mark kept walking, but the Lord spoke to his heart again and said, "Mark, I want you to go tell that man I love him." So Mark went to the van and said to the other men, "God just spoke to my heart. I'm supposed to go tell that man God loves him. Who wants to go with me?" They all said God didn't tell them anything, so they weren't budging. Mark said, "Okay, you guys wait here. And pray for me."

Mark walked up to the big fellow, tapped him on the shoulder, and said, "Sir, I know you are going to think I'm crazy, but I'm a Christian, and I walked by you just a minute ago, and God spoke to me and told me to tell you He loves you. So I just want you to know that God loves you. Good night."

Mark turned to walk away, but then the big fellow collapsed to his knees and started weeping! The man was obviously hurting, so Mark laid his hand on the man's shoulder and tried to comfort him. The other college men saw what was happening, and they left the van to gather around the big fellow too.

The man continued weeping, and eventually he said to Mark, "I have a loaded revolver in my pocket. I was sitting at the bar drinking, thinking about what a waste my life has been. And for some reason I prayed, 'God if You love me then tell me, because if You don't . . .' ".

When the man walked out of the bar, he had leaned against that telephone pole to think about where he would go to shoot himself. Over the next several minutes, Mark and the other men prayed with this broken man and led him to Christ.

Notes from Benny's Journal
"GOD'S MESSENGER"

One Sunday afternoon God began speaking to my heart about a friend. When that happens, I immediately pray for that person. As I prayed, I knew I had to go see my friend. He lived in a distant state, so I told Marilou that I was booking a flight to leave early the next morning.

After a very early flight, I arrived at my friend's place of business as it was opening for the day. When I saw his secretary, she had a pale look on her face. I asked if my friend was there, and she informed me that he had had a stroke that morning and was rushed to the hospital.

I spent the rest of that day with him in his hospital room serving him, encouraging his wife and children, and praying. Even though he couldn't talk, I seemed to understand his groans and knew what he was requesting. Later, my friend was able to confirm that I was actually hearing what God understood his needs to be. Many times that day, his wife and children said to me, "You know God sent you here today, don't you?"

Wouldn't it be great if we all could have stories like this to tell? Well, we can! Watching God work miracles in the lives of people He calls us to touch ought to be a way of life for us, but it takes courage—because the more we respond to God, the more He will work through us. The greater the miracle God wants to perform, the greater the challenge will often be to retreat to our comfort zone.

True People of Prayer

Prayer should be a way of life—perhaps even a state of mind. We can all get into the habit of using prayer as a life management tool—a way of tapping into God's provision for our needs and anxieties. That's not necessarily wrong; God tells us to call on Him for our daily needs and the needs of others, and we should do that.

But prayer is more than treating God as the great Santa in the sky. He knows your need even before you tell Him. Paul instructs us in Philippians 4:6 how to make our requests known to God, and Jesus shows us in Matthew 6:9–13 how to pray when we talk directly to God. But what about other times? What about the times when we aren't in our prayer times or worshiping God in church? Do we forget when we are working, playing, eating, and coming and going that we are still in God's presence? The fact is, we're always in the midst of heaven. That's right! Heaven isn't some far-off distant place—it's the presence of God in His own kingdom.

Is there anywhere or anything that God is not king of? No, God is everywhere and His kingdom includes everything. You are living and moving in the midst of God and His angels at all times. Being born again allows for that. One preacher likes to say that Christians are multidimensional beings. Simultaneously, we walk upon the earth, and we walk in the midst of heaven (Ephesians 2:6).

We can sharpen our awareness of God's kingdom by listening for God to speak, by watching for Him to act, and most of all, by being ready to respond in faith when God speaks. As Jesus told Nicodemus, we can see the kingdom of God (John 3:3). That ought to be the way we live every day.

A person of prayer is not self-reliant. It isn't through strong, self-reliant people that God's strength is shown. It is through the things we don't have the strength to do that God brings glory to Himself. We give ourselves and our impossible tasks to God, and He somehow makes them perfect. Paul says he even bragged about how weak he was so God's strength was all the more glorious:

And [the Lord] said to me, "My grace is sufficient for you, for My strength is made perfect in weakness." Therefore most gladly I will rather boast in my infirmities, that the power of Christ may rest upon me.

Therefore I take pleasure in infirmities, in reproaches, in needs, in perse-cutions, in distresses, for Christ's sake. For when I am weak, then I am strong. 2 Corinthians 12:9–10 (NKJV)

Being people who pray is different from being people *of* prayer. Nearly 95 percent of all people say they pray, and all followers of Jesus pray at times. People *of* prayer are glad to be totally dependant on God at all times, because that's when they are able to hear Him. There is nothing more life changing than knowing you are actually hearing God.

> *People of prayer walk with God every day—all day.*

People of prayer walk with God every day—all day. They talk to Him, they hear from Him, and they do what He says. It is more than a random experience. Their constant awareness of God's presence has become a way of life. Living this way changes them from the inside out. Their walk in a continual attitude of prayer makes them who they are (Romans 12:12; Colossians 4:2).

check point

Think about your life in the last twenty-four hours—the various things that happened and the people you saw.

Now, in relation to your daily life, make a list of some ways you can become more aware of the fact that God is always with you—ways that will draw your attention to Him.

Here are some ways that help me remember God is always with me:

1. When I wake up in the morning and I'm still lying in my bed, the first things I try to do are pray and acknowledge that God is with me.

2. When I suddenly begin thinking about someone, I assume God is bringing them to my mind, and I try to pray for them immediately.

3. Every time I look at a clock, it's a reminder to think about God's continuous love for me and His presence in me. I remember that God is with me, minute by minute.

4. When I see the number four, it's my chosen symbol that God is always at work "4" me. You may have a different number that is special to you.

5. I choose to believe God is concerned about everything in my life, no matter how insignificant it may seem. I try to pray about everything.

6. I try to follow the plan laid out in William Sheldon's book, *In His Steps*. When I am making a decision, I count to ten in my mind and ask myself, *What would Jesus do?* Then I try to do it.

chapter ten

God-centered parents are people of faith

how do I actively permit God to rule over my life?

A VIEW OF THE ROAD AHEAD:

- *Admitting faith isn't about luck*
- *Increasing faith*

My personal definition of faith means giving God permission to run my life. When your God is big, your problems are small. When your God is small, your problems are big. It all depends on how big your view of God is and whether or not you believe He cares or even exists.

Today, the idea of living by faith is under attack. Now, more than any other time in history, teenagers are encouraged by culture to trust only in themselves for fulfillment. This has been a growing trend since the end of World War II. Our culture in general, and youth in particular, seems to have outgrown the need to put trust in God.

For more than two generations now, faith in God has been undermined by scientific biases propagated by people who don't seek the truth, but rather only want a society void of any accountability to God for their actions or expressions. If there is no God and we are a product of evolutionary luck, then there is no wrong or right. Every man is now dependent on himself to define what is true and what is fantasy. Moral boundaries are no more than an ever-changing state of mind, and God is just an imaginary figure who replaces the void left by those things science has yet to discover.

> *If there is no God and we are a product of evolutionary luck, then there is no wrong or right.*

It's more fashionable than ever among youth not to trust their parents or respect other authority figures. This trend reminds me of when Paul warns of the perilous times when people will be lovers of themselves rather than lovers of God (2 Timothy 3:1–5). Faith is often viewed as no more than blind luck; it's rejected as an ignorant step into the dark during what should be an age of enlightenment. What an arrogant lie!

Characteristics of God-Centered People

God-centered parents desire to show their children a different way. They know faith in God is not blind luck; it's an intelligent choice. God revealing Himself in creation, in history, and in His Son Jesus Christ is the best documented and most reliable truth available (Romans 1:20).

Faith in the God who revealed Himself in Christ is the only sure foundation of life, hope, and peace, and history has proven that. God-centered parents desire to live by faith day by day, trusting God in everything. They know God is trustworthy and is able to do far more good in their lives than they could ever accomplish on their own. God is Lord regardless of man's opinion, and He rules and reigns over everything according to His own will.

A God-centered person of faith obeys God because he or she *wants* God to be in control. They actively permit God to lead them in every area of their life (Proverbs 3:4–6). The immediate advantage of God-centered faith over self-centered control is that it provides a wellspring of hope, inner peace, and the freedom to love.

Another characteristic of God-centered people of faith is that they understand God will sometimes call on them to attempt things that may seem impossible. Hebrews 11 says, "Without faith it is impossible to please God"(NIV). If you don't trust God, you can't please Him. If you don't submit your life to God, you can't please Him. If you don't believe God can do more than you can, you can't please Him.

Many Christians say, "God, I'll do for You everything I can do." But it doesn't require faith to do what *we* can do; faith is asking God what *He* desires to do and then asking Him to use us in doing it. God will give people of faith something they can't do, and then through His strength they'll go do it. That's another part of the great adventure; they overcome their fear and unbelief with faith in God. That's what's pleases Him.

Notes from Benny's Journal
"A LOOK AT AMERICA"

I knew God was calling me to greater faith and that He wanted me to learn more of what it meant to live by faith. So in 1998, I committed to God to become a man of faith. In early April, as I began this pursuit, the Lord began to speak to me in a reoccurring dream. In this dream, I was to take a year of my life, travel to all fifty states, and take a look at America through the eyes of our youth. As I went through the process of confirming that it was God speaking and then surrendering to this call, it was already June. God had placed an impossible task before me! It was to happen in 1999.

*Following His design, I had six months to assemble a team of fifty people who would put their lives on hold and commit an entire year to travel with me. In addition, I was to raise one million dollars to complete the task. I knew it would take a miracle. In my book, **A Look at America**, I tell the entire story. But it did happen! It was exciting, scary, and overwhelming, and the greatest struggle I ever faced. At the same time, it was the greatest adventure I've ever experienced. God gave me an impossible dream. My family, fifty others, and I responded in faith, and the dream became a reality.*

I am still on that precious, perilous journey, and I'm still learning.

Don't Miss Out

Many people have dreams but don't practice a life of faith, so they never really see what God can do through them. I wanted to be a part of something God did that is bigger than me. The faith hall of fame in Hebrews, chapter 11, is about people who accomplished the impossible with nothing more than complete trust in God.

Do you really trust God? Do you face challenges and difficulties with dread, even though God has always brought you through them in the past? You don't have to condemn yourself if you do; we all get frustrated with life in this world. But you can ask God to help you use life as an opportunity to see Him work. Faith, like everything else we get from God, is a gift. He gives it proportionately, according to our needs and our dreams. Ask the Holy Spirit to give you more faith and to replace your dread with anticipation of the joy you'll feel when God works His purposes in and through you.

There are five words in Scripture that I don't like: "O ye of little faith." I like them even less when I find myself in times of confusion and doubt. Jesus used them many times to explain our anxiety over uncertainty.

We often react to circumstances as if God is distant or out of control. When we can't see God at work or don't understand His ways, we can find ourselves feeling overwhelmed. But God is faithful; His nature and character constant. When we are walking in the Spirit, seeking God in worship, studying His Word, and praying continually, our faith will be stronger and will continue to grow.

check
point

1. Make a list of the things you know God wants you to do. Include your present responsibilities and callings, as well as the things you think God may be calling you to in the future.

2. Now make a list of the dreams—great and small—that you believe God has planted in you.

3. God promises to give you the faith to accomplish everything He gives you to do. Pray for God to strengthen your faith in Him and help you apply it to all His commands, as well as your challenges and dreams. Begin every day with this prayer for your children and yourself.

> *Father God, I need You to guide my life today. Help me see my life and its circumstances as opportunities for You to be strong in me and work through me.*
>
> *Teach me to joyfully expect Your presence in me and in everything that happens today—good or bad. Let my growing faith in You guard me against fear and doubt.*
>
> *Reveal to me the things You want me to do. Let the dreams You have placed in my life be limited only by Your will, not by who I am.*
>
> *Give me the faith I need to do the things You have called me to do. Strengthen me to accomplish the dreams You have given me.*
>
> *God, You provide the power, and I, as your faithful servant and highly favored child, will simply obey. Teach me to live by faith.*
>
> *Teach me to live assured of what I hope for and certain of what I cannot see. Amen.*

chapter eleven

God-centered parents are people of hope

how can I share the hope of Jesus with my children?

A VIEW OF THE ROAD AHEAD:

- *Anticipating God's promises*
- *Understanding hope*

We don't hope as the world hopes. People of the world only hope for what may or may not happen. Teenagers may hope they'll get to drive when they turn sixteen, but they may not be able to pass the test. Adults may be hoping and striving for a better job or a better house, but they may not get those things. We hope our team will win the game, but they might lose.

A Different Kind of Hope

The hope Christians experience is a different hope altogether. We don't have to think about whether God's promises might or might not happen. We can enjoy the anticipation that they are going to happen. We dream about *when*, not *if*. We don't think about *if* Christ is coming again;

our kind of hope anticipates *when* He is coming again. This kind of hope influences our everyday lives in a positive way.

Peter asked us to consider, since Christ is coming back, what kind of lives we should be living (see 2 Peter 3:10–13). Judging by Peter's remarks, he was writing to people who he knew were certain of Christ's coming; there was no need to convince them. His argument was that this certainty should make their lives different from the lives of people who hope for things without any certainty.

For example, compare our hope of eternal life with what happens on a couple's wedding day. Imagine a bride finally hearing her groom say the words "I do" and the minister sealing the couple's vows by pronouncing them husband and wife. The tremendous joy the couple feels in those heart-pounding moments is derived from finally possessing the promised family they both had hoped for. Before the wedding, they had hope, but it was different because their hope for a life together was anticipated yet not guaranteed. After the vows are sealed and the marriage is recognized as final, the couple has certain possession of the thing for which they hoped. The certainty of it is in their hands.

This is the kind of hope all Christians have right now with Christ, our Bridegroom. We aren't waiting for vows to be said; Jesus has already said His vows. They were written in His Word for the whole world to witness. As the Bride of Christ, we have given our vows by receiving Christ and keeping ourselves only unto Him. The main difference between our hope in Christ and the realized hope of married couples is that our hope is eternal; our joy will never end. Married couples know the joy of their hope will end eventually in death; sadly, it can also be destroyed by divorce.

As God's chosen family, we have the only kind of hope that is certain and eternal.

As God's chosen family, we have the only kind of hope that is certain and eternal. We aren't waiting for the hope of spending eternity with Jesus, as if it might or might not happen (1 John 5:11–13). Our faith in

Jesus' life, death, and resurrection assures us that we have already been given to Him by the Father (John 10:28–29). We are His; He will never leave us or forsake us (Hebrews 13:5). It is this assured hope that Jesus wants us to share with all the world (Matthew 28:18–20).

We can't just keep our joy in Christ to ourselves. Belonging to Jesus means we are free from the kind of anxiety and uncertainty that others live with every day. The rest of the world is full of masked fears about the future; they have no assured hope to give them real joy and real peace. Jesus is the answer; He is the only hope of the world. It is through the hope-filled lives of our Christian families that we have the most effective way to share the love of Christ with the world.

Notes from Benny's Journal
"A LOVE TO REMEMBER"

When I was a youth pastor, I often ran into young adults who had gone through my ministry years earlier. They would thank me for the impact I had on their lives, and I would ask them to tell me what we did that made a difference in them. I was thinking it might be something I taught them or something we did together.

To my surprise, it was not in my great theological insight or my superior programs; usually they could remember only a few things I had said. The overwhelming majority said it was my family and the way I loved my wife and my children. Some have told me they always wanted a family like that.

Obviously, they didn't live in our house 24/7, or they would have seen the rough times too, but Christ was being glorified and reflected in our home enough to draw them to Him.

The Scripture says it is a wise man who wins souls. I've heard many spiritual teachers say, "Preach all the time; speak when necessary." I've also heard it said, "Your life is speaking so loud, I can't hear what you are saying!" Jesus commanded us not just to *live* it, but also to *tell* His story to everyone. John the disciple wrote that those who have Christ have life,

Know Jesus, know hope.

No Jesus, no hope.

and those who don't have Christ are dead already (John 3:36). Christ is our only hope! People of hope share Jesus.

We cannot be people of hope if we are not living and sharing Jesus. There is no hope apart from Him. Know Jesus, know hope. No Jesus, no hope.

 **check** point

First Peter 3:15 says we should be ready at all times to give an account for the hope that is in us; but we are commanded to do it with gentleness and respect.

We should be able to support and defend our position in a debate about things like the reliability of the Bible, creation versus evolution, Christ's fulfillment of prophecy, and so on. But proving our point won't necessarily give people hope. We need to tell them about freedom from guilt, why we have no fear about life after death, why we have joy that the world can't take away, and why we have meaningful purpose in this life and the life to come.

We need to help them understand that God is not just concerned about following the rules; He is seeking a loving relationship that has eternal benefits. Our children need our help to come into a relationship with God so that they may also have the assurance of eternal life. We can help them begin their journey toward Christlikeness.

A good way to prepare yourself to share these things with others is to understand this lesson about hope. Seek God's wisdom so you can learn how to tell people about this hope in a way that touches the soft spots in their lives; try to understand what they really care about, what their hurts and pains are, what their needs and concerns are. You can't promise people the world, but you can promise them life. We must help lost and troubled people see that Jesus is the way, the truth, and the life they are longing for.

Here are some things you can do to step up your efforts in sharing your hope in Christ:

1. Repent and turn away from anything that would keep you from being a reflection of Christ.

2. List the people in your family and circle of friends who need to know Jesus.

3. Pray for God to open the door for conversations about Christ, and when He does, tell people what Christ means to you.

4. Show the love of Christ through thoughtful words and deeds.

5. Ask your pastor for a Christian book on sharing your faith.

6. Find a gospel tract you can use to help you share with someone.

chapter twelve

God-centered parents are people of love

how can I love the way God loves?

A VIEW OF THE ROAD AHEAD:

- *Feeling God's unconditional love*
- *Sacrificing all for love*

The final pursuit of God-centered parents is one that best reflects God's character. It is the most fundamental pursuit, so I've saved it for last. We can't even begin to imitate God without practicing love the way He does.

Paul says if we don't have the Spirit of Godlike love, then every other thing we have is pointless. Without love, it doesn't matter how much we are filled and empowered by the Spirit, how much faith, hope, and knowledge of the Word we have, or how much we worship and pray (1 Corinthians 13). Everything not rooted in love is lifeless and colorless.

Even with all the novels, poetry, music, and films about love, our culture is still confused about the true definition of love. We tend to measure how much we love someone by how we *feel*. In contrast, we tend to measure how much others love us by what they *do* for us.

True Love

The focus of what God calls love isn't about feeling or receiving. The focus of true love is God Himself. While the world says "all you need is love," love is not God—God is love (1 John 4:16); His very nature is to love.

True love is something we do. It has everything to do with giving. God loves a cheerful giver because He is a cheerful giver. John 3:16 says

> The focus of true love is God Himself.

that God so loved that He gave. When we give cheerfully out of love, we are reflecting His nature in us. When you love like God, you are benefiting someone else at your expense. The greater a sacrifice is, the greater it is a work of love. The less deserving of love someone is the more Godlike is the love given to them.

God is pleased when we love this way because it is a reflection of who God is at the center of His heart. When we love others His way, God receives it as love given personally to Him (Matthew 25:31–46).

Unfortunately, our culture relies too much on the words "I love you." Of course we all want to hear the words, but they would be dead and meaningless to us from people who never demonstrate their love sacrificially. We do the same thing with blessings. Instead of blessing someone's life, we often make do with words like "God bless you" or "bless your heart." It's sort of a joke that in the South we can safely say just about any insulting thing we want to someone, as long as we add the words "bless your heart!".

We soften the impact of the insult with cheap words of goodwill. That's because words are cheap without action. Nowhere in Scripture is it recorded that Jesus ever put His arm around someone and said, "I love you." He talked about His love and the love of the Father, but we have no record that He ever said those three words directly to someone.

The Ultimate Sacrifice

We trust that love was the foundation of what Jesus did for us because of His loving sacrifices. Jesus gave His life for us; it cost Him everything to give us everything. He was the sovereign King of eternity and all creation. He became worse than nothing, the bearer of all sin, so that we, His enemies (Romans 5:10), could receive His righteousness. And with His resurrection, He made us joint heirs with Him to His kingdom. Joint inheritance means Jesus inherits nothing unless we inherit as well.

We can't even begin to imagine the level of sacrifice in His love. That's another reason why we already have our eternal life.

People of Godlike love and blessing aim to bring good into some-one's life, and they give no thought to themselves. Parents are able to understand this better than anyone else. When we have our first child, we get our first personal glimpse into how God loves us. Suddenly, we value someone else's life above our own. We are willing to pay any cost to benefit our children. But in a way, benefiting our children indirectly benefits us. Everyone we know also knows our chil-dren, and if our children look good, we look good. It's the sacrifices of love that promise no return which bring the most glory to God.

When we have our first child, we get our first personal glimpse into how God loves us.

Darryl Scott tells a story about an act of sacrificial love performed by his daughter, Rachel. A few weeks before she was murdered at Columbine High School, she helped a man who was struggling with a flat tire on the side of a rain-soaked highway. Rachel was a small slip of a girl, but she instinctively pulled over to offer help. She didn't have much strength to offer, but she held an umbrella over the man and handed him tools while he changed the tire. Afterwards, the man thanked Rachel for her kindness and they parted. Weeks later, at the end of Rachel's funeral, there was an altar call. One of the many people who came forward to give their lives to Christ was the man Rachel had shown kindness to.

Of all the things through which God can work miracles, the most powerful is sacrificial love. Rachel Scott's diaries and lifestyle show that everything she did came from a broken-hearted love for lost souls. That act of compassion on a rainy afternoon only cost Rachel a little time and attention to a man's momentary struggle. God used it to draw the man's attention to Rachel's testimony about the love of Jesus Christ.

check point

There is no way that a loveless heart can be trained to love; but a God-seeking, Spirit-led follower of Christ has the advantage of a promise.

If a Christian dares to follow Christ out of love for Him, Christ will fill that follower with His own love for the world. The Holy Spirit puts God's love in our hearts.

1. How did Christ's love for all mankind show that He put their needs before His own?

2. Putting the needs and well-being of others before our own are true reflections of God and His love. Name three people you know who live that way, and give an example of how they have shown sacrificial love.

3. Take a few moments and write a note to the people you listed above, telling them how their example has impacted your life. Even if the person is no longer living, write the note anyway. Send it to their nearest relative to share the blessing of that person's life with them (see

Ephesians 2:1–10: God doesn't make bad people good, God makes dead people alive).

4. God does not try to improve our old hearts; He gives us new ones. Read 2 Corinthians 5:17, and then describe the difference in your new heart as compared to your old heart.

a worthy pursuit
where do I go from here?

Working through this book has been a long journey in pursuit of the timeless treasures of God. In fact, the seven pursuits of God-centered parents are a way of life that we should pass on to our children; they're lessons that will continue throughout eternity. We'll never come to the place where no more growth is possible, because God will continually astonish us with something new to reveal (1 Corinthians 2:9).

In heaven, the seven pursuits will still be part of our everyday life. God's Word and the mysteries of faith, hope, and love will always be fresh paths to travel. Our prayers will be face-to-face encounters with God. Worship will celebrate our continually growing adoration and understanding of God's love. Our presence with Jesus as King of heaven and our unlimited intimacy with the Spirit will fully satisfy a much greater longing for God than we have now.

The value of all these pursuits is in the value of God Himself. We are pursuing God. As people of the Spirit, the Word, worship, prayer, faith, hope, and love, we become people of God. And the exciting thing is that while pursuing God, we are actually opening the door wider for Him to pursue us. This doesn't mean we will always know how He is pursuing us, but we can trust that He always will—even when we fail in our pursuit of Him.

The study of the seven pursuits was mainly intended to be an admonition for parents though. Unless we pursue the things of God while our children are with us, becoming like God could be a much more difficult journey for them as Christian adults. We must model for our children the single, most important pursuit of our lives—a growing relationship with God through Jesus Christ—while making sure they understand our devotion to the seven pursuits.

To become a whole person with the loving character of God, your constant attitude of prayer should look something like this:

Father, I ask, like Jesus, not to think less of myself, but to think of myself less. I surrender my will, my body, and my heart to Your use in loving my family, my fellow Christians, and the world.

You must have Christlike humility to be a God-centered parent. There will be stages in your children's lives when they will desire to journey with you, and there will be stages when they'll need to go it alone. Don't give in to fear or impatience; if you humbly submit to His leading, the Spirit can make you attentive to how He is moving in your children's hearts. But in every way you enter your child's heart and life, let your love and fearless hope in Christ lead you. Ultimately, pursuing the things of God is about being transformed into the image of God. That's what we want for ourselves as parents, because that's what we want for our children.

A Worthy Challenge

The journey of pursuing the character of Christ isn't a walk in the park. The road we travel is flanked by deceitful distractions and destructive forces. They are made powerful by the desires that originate in our sinful nature. The home of our sin nature is often referred to as *the flesh.*

- Our flesh will run from God or will ignore Him and try to draw us to the side of the road where it finds the things it wants.
- Our flesh will want to stand on opinions.
- Our flesh will want to be self-reliant and try to find fulfillment in the world.
- Our flesh will serve itself before others and hope only in what it controls.
- Our flesh will desire to reach for satisfaction in ways that are against God's will and damaging to us.
- Our flesh is like a spoiled child, and it must have a strong parent to train it.

We can learn to master our flesh and guard our hearts in the trustworthy presence and strength of the Holy Spirit. Trusting God's unconditional love and learning to walk in the Spirit are the keys to daily success in the seven pursuits of Christlikeness.

Life Isn't Supposed to Be Perfect

One thing that made my journey easier and more peaceful was learning to accept the fact that there would always be peaks and valleys in my spiritual life, times when prayer would come easily and times when it would be difficult.

I had to accept that sometimes I wouldn't be able to satisfy my hunger for reading the Bible, while other times, it would be hard to even pick it up. If our spiritual lives are bells, then sometimes they'll sing like the bells in cathedral towers, while other times, they'll sound like hollow logs. It's easier to practice the seven pursuits when our spirits ring loud and true.

The Christian life is about pursuing God, not pursuing a perfect life.

But God actually does His best work in us during the rough times. The rough times remind us that we're broken souls with bodies of dust.

The Christian life is about pursuing God, not pursuing a perfect life. And remember that when you are pursuing God, it is really *God* who is pursuing *you*.

Taking Inventory

Why is it so difficult at times to consistently read the Bible, pray, and pursue the things that will help us grow? There are four obstacles that slow our growth in Christ and make our pursuit of God's character more difficult, and any of us can be troubled by them:

1. Pursuing God with the wrong attitude
2. The presence of sin in our lives
3. Putting our comfort and safety first
4. Feeling that God isn't present in our lives

Identifying these obstacles can provide us with a checklist to take account of our spiritual lives when they seem unusually difficult.

Pursuing God with the Wrong Attitude

Practicing the seven pursuits because you fear God's displeasure will soon become a meaningless effort. Instead of the blessing the pursuits are intended to be, they'll be a burden in your life. Or if the seven pursuits are simply a way to gain favor and acceptance with God, you will gain very little from your efforts. The activity will be a legalistic routine in which God finds no pleasure. You must pursue God's character out of desire for Him and with faith that He desires you unconditionally. With this attitude, the seven pursuits will become very attractive to you. They will consume your thoughts and become a way of life for you (John 10:10).

The Presence of Sin in Your Life

Putting other things above our desire to know and serve God is idolatry that replaces our passionate pursuit of God. In the last chapter, you identified these areas and made a vow to address them. You know how

God feels about your idolatry—it's similar to the way you would feel about discovering adultery in your spouse. The difference is that in spite of our unfaithfulness, God will keep His commitment to love and disciple us.

But our sin will bring disruption to our spiritual life because we aren't depending on Him alone for our strength, wisdom, and life. If you find it very difficult to pray, and reading the Bible gives you anxiety, it may be time to take inventory of all the things to which you are giving your life.

Putting Your Comfort and Safety First

When we find ourselves in a place of unbroken comfort and contentment in our lives, we are most likely not pursuing the things of God. We are probably evading the inconvenience and disruption to our lives that ministry opportunities often bring. Jesus told us that *if we follow Him,* the world will bring us tribulation. But He also promised that He has overcome the world (John 16:33).

If you find your spiritual life becoming dry and uninspired, consider that you may have stepped out of the adventure. Adventure means risking and exploring new territory. It also means trusting God to carry you through disruptions and even failures.

Feeling God Isn't Present in Your Life

When God seems to be silent, He is still present in our lives and He will answer our prayers. He doesn't always make His presence and answers known though. Many times we must wait to see how God is working. Most of what God is doing in our lives we won't be able to understand until we are in heaven. Our reaction to God's silence can be a barometer of our level of trust in and surrender to Him. Not having all the answers to our needs when and how we want them can cause great anxiety. The obstacle to our spiritual growth happens when we react badly to the anxiety.

The question for us is this: do we trust God so much that we can celebrate His love for us even when our lives are full of unwelcome things that God seems to be silent about? You can expect to go through periods of need or unusual difficulty in your life during which you won't receive any reassurance from God, in spite of increased time pursuing Him. If you've taken inventory and you're confident that God's silence isn't discipline for something, then just accept that He is at work in you at a deeper level where only His silence can reach. Rest in what you know about how God loves and accepts you. He is always at work in your life behind the scenes. But sometimes He wants to strengthen your ability to rest on what you know about Him instead of how often you hear from Him.

The View from the Summit

In this book, we've been on an expedition to the mountain of God. We began by looking at the challenge before us. I showed you the challenge I was given to follow my parent's example, we discovered how God renews our spiritual needs and equips us to fight against the enemy, and we charted our course to becoming God-centered parents.

We have now reached the summit and found that God's Spirit was in front of us all the time. We have learned what it means to live by the Spirit. But the journey isn't over! We can't stay on the summit. We must be led back down the mountain to the valley below where we live in the world.

Through the seven pursuits, we'll journey frequently with the Spirit back to the mountain of God to be restored and inspired with fresh vision. But over time, we'll become increasingly aware that our life in the Spirit has two sides: at the same time the Spirit is leading us closer to God through our relationship with Jesus, He is also leading us to follow Jesus into a battle. It's a battle that has already been won, but we must learn to stand firmly on the true source of this victory.

Now, commit to becoming the person God created you to be. Begin using the seven pursuits of God-centered parents to chart the course of your daily life—not just as a parent, but as a child of God.

our mission

Our mission is reaching and discipling the next generation for Jesus Christ.

our vision

First Priority is a city vision shared by local churches to build a comprehensive strategy and provide relevant resources that will encourage, equip, and empower students, parents, leaders, and churches to unite within the community and on campus to care for and to disciple a generation for Jesus Christ.

If you want more information about First Priority, visit our Web site at www.fpoa.org

Or you can write to us at:

First Priority of America, Inc.
115 Penn Warren Drive, Suite 300-205
Nashville, TN 37027